FOR THE GREATEST GOOD

EARLY HISTORY OF THE GIFFORD PINCHOT NATIONAL FOREST

RICK MCCLURE AND CHERYL MACK

LYNN SCHINNELL, EDITOR

"For the Greatest Good"
Early History of Gifford Pinchot National Forest

JULY 1, 2008 MARKS THE CENTENNIAL OF PRESIDENT THEODORE ROOSEVELT'S EXECUTIVE ORDER CREATING THE COLUMBIA NATIONAL FOREST, RENAMED GIFFORD PINCHOT NATIONAL FOREST IN HONOR OF THE FIRST CHIEF OF THE U.S. FOREST SERVICE. THIS BOOK CHRONICLES THE EARLY HISTORY OF THE FOREST UP TO 1949.

RANGER HARVEY LICKEL HOISTS THE FLAG AT GOTCHEN CREEK RANGER STATION IN 1910. PHOTO BY COLUMBIA NATIONAL FOREST SUPERVISOR H.O. STABLER.

For the Greatest Good: Early History of Gifford Pinchot National Forest
by Rick McClure and Cheryl Mack
Edited by Lynn Schinnell

Northwest Interpretive Association
Copyright © 1999, 2008
Second Edition 2008

Published by
Northwest Interpretive Association
164 South Jackson Street, Seattle, WA 98104
www.nwpubliclands.org

ISBN-10   0-914019-59-7
ISBN-13   978-0-914019-59-6

Printed in the United States of America

Northwest Interpretive Association (NWIA) is a 501(c)(3) nonprofit corporation based in Seattle, Washington and licensed to operate in Oregon, Idaho, California, and Montana. For more than 30 years NWIA has provided resources to promote enhanced enjoyment and understanding of Northwest public lands. Through partnerships with the USDA Forest Service, National Park Service, US Army Corps of Engineers, Washington State Parks, City of Seattle Public Utilities, and Bureau of Reclamation NWIA acts as a crucial supporter of public lands, helping to educate visitors by providing valuable information about the lands we all share in common. For more information, please visit our website at **www.nwpubliclands.org.**

Book and Cover Design by Ben Nechanicky

A. B. CONRAD (RIGHT) AND UNIDENTIFIED FOREST GUARD PREPARE TO HEAD UP THE LEWIS RIVER TRAIL, ca. 1910

RANGER STATION AT COPPER CITY CAMP, ca. 1925

CONTENTS

Acknowlegments

We are indebted to Kirk P. Cecil, Forest Supervisor from 1933 through 1949 for his efforts to collect and compile historical information about the Gifford Pinchot National Forest. In the late 1930s, Cecil asked his rangers to interview local old timers and prepare written historical summaries of their districts. During the 1940s Cecil contacted and corresponded with many of the early forest rangers and guards, asking them to provide recollections of their experiences. Several excerpts have been included in this book. We have also drawn liberally from a notebook of personnel data compiled by Cecil in 1964.

We would also like to express our gratitude to Barbara Hollenbeck, Forest Archaeologist for the Gifford Pinchot National Forest from 1980 to 1991, for her efforts to preserve many of the documents and photographs we have used for this book. Our appreciation is also extended to Jamie Tolfree and Susan Whitney, former employees of the Wind River Nursery, for their efforts to collect and care for archival materials from the nursery.

The authors would also like to thank Becky Philpot of Grey Towers National Historic Landmark, Jerry Williams, Laura Backlund, Jan Hollenbeck, and Mary Rakestraw for contributing materials that appear in this book.

Thanks also to Candace Lein-Hayes of the National Archives North Pacific Branch in Seattle for her assistance in locating some of the oldest documents pertaining to the history of this forest.

This publication is the result of a wonderful partnership and collaboration between Gifford Pinchot National Forest and Northwest Interpretive Association. The second edition was made possible through the support of Executive Director Jim Adams and the editorial guidance of Ben Nechanicky.

A Message from the Forest Supervisor

A century ago, President Theodore Roosevelt signed the executive order creating the Columbia National Forest, later renamed to honor Gifford Pinchot, first Chief of the Forest Service. In 2008, we celebrate the lasting importance of this place. From the craggy peaks and high trails of the Goat Rocks, the recovering volcanic landscapes of Mount St. Helens, and the dazzling glaciers of Mt. Adams, to the swift rapids of Cowlitz, Cispus, Toutle, and Wind Rivers, this place is the heartbeat of the Cascades.

In this centennial year we remember the people, places, and events that have shaped our history. Honoring the work of those that came before, and the purposes our forest has served in the past, reminds us that the work of today will become the traditions of tomorrow. The principles of conservation established by Gifford Pinchot remain at the foundation of what we do today in caring for this land and managing it to best meet the needs of all people.

The Gifford Pinchot National Forest today is a place of abundance. We continue to protect this special place for its lasting legacy; we learn from it. The optimism and resiliency of this natural world leaves us all with a hopeful message for the future.

Claire Lavendel
Gifford Pinchot National Forest Supervisor, 1999—Present

A Book of Memories

Personal recollections. Worn and faded black-and-white photographs. Journal entries from the first expeditions. Frayed letters from early rangers. Field notes.

Spread before you, these pieces create a portrait of Gifford Pinchot National Forest's history.

This book is an attempt to look at the history of Gifford Pinchot National Forest through the eyes of the people who shaped it. First-person accounts and photographs are scattered throughout the pages.

This is not a comprehensive history, but rather a quick glimpse of the forest's early days. Look back through the eyes of the Indians, fur traders, explorers, and rangers to gain an understanding of the land we call Gifford Pinchot National Forest.

Gifford Pinchot National Forest

Gifford Pinchot National Forest has been known by many names since its creation as a forest reserve over a century ago—Pacific Forest Reserve, Mount Rainier Forest Reserve, Rainier National Forest, Columbia National Forest, and finally as Gifford Pinchot National Forest. Today Gifford Pinchot National Forest encompasses an area of 1,527,761 acres in south-central Washington State.

This rugged, mountainous landscape is drained by the Cowlitz, Toutle, Lewis, Wind, Little White Salmon, and White Salmon Rivers and dominated by two volcanoes—Mount Adams (12,276 feet elevation) and Mount St. Helens (7,877 feet elevation).

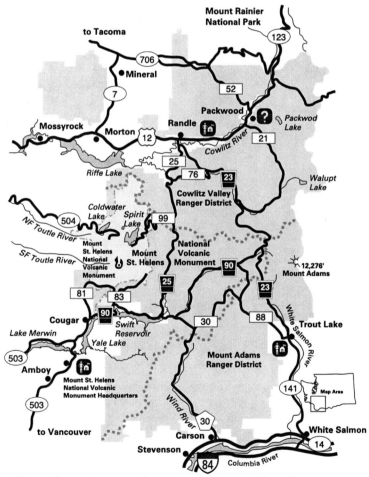

map shows National Forest administrative boundaries as of printing of this publication

"Conservation to Gifford Pinchot is not a vague, fuzzy aspiration. It was something concrete, exact, dynamic. The application of science and technology to our material economy for the purpose of enhancing and elevating the life of the individual. The very stuff of which democracy is made. The Conservation he preached dealt not only with trees but the sheep herders and homesteaders, whose means of livelihood in the forest depended upon the kind of protection that could be given them."

—*Cornelia Pinchot (widow of Gifford Pinchot)*
from a speech at La Wis Wis Forest Camp, October 15, 1949

GIFFORD PINCHOT 1865-1946

The Father of Conservationism

Gifford Pinchot was the first professional forester in America and the first chief of the U. S. Forest Service.

Pinchot was born in Pennsylvania in 1865. He attended Yale University. Because there were no courses in forestry available in the United States at that time, Pinchot traveled to France and studied under European foresters.

He returned to the United States at the age of 25, taking up a career as a professional forester.

In 1891 he was hired to manage the 7,000-acre Vanderbilt estate in North Carolina. In 1893 he opened an office in New York City as a consulting forester.

In 1896 the National Academy of Sciences appointed Pinchot to a special National Forest Commission. The commissioners traveled west to examine public lands under consideration as forest reserves.

After the trip, Pinchot prepared a description of Mt. Rainier Forest Reserve and other proposed forest reserves, which were created the following year by President Cleveland.

Pinchot brought the Yale Forestry School to the area in the summer of 1899. The students conducted field studies along the upper Nisqually River. This may have been the only time Pinchot set foot in what is now part of Gifford Pinchot National Forest.

Pinchot was named chief of the 10-person Division of Forestry in 1898, within the Department of Agriculture, under President McKinley's administration.

Initially, the Division of Forestry had no public lands under its jurisdiction. The forest reserves were administered by the Department of the Interior, General Land Office.

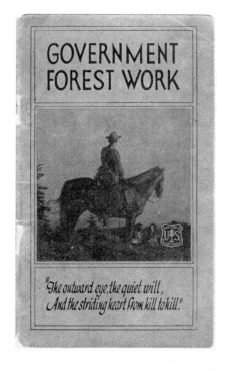

It was Pinchot's dream to shift these lands to the Department of Agriculture. In 1905, it finally happened. The U. S. Forest Service was created, with Pinchot at the helm.

Pinchot served as Chief Forester of the U.S. Forest Service from 1905 to 1910.

"The fight for conservation, exactly as the fight for Democracy, must be reinvigorated, revived, remanned, re-vitalized by each succeeding generation. Its implications, its urgencies, its logistics, translated in terms of their own day by each generation. Conservation is still a philosphy of dynamic humanism. Still to be conceived in relation not only to science and techniques, but primarily in relation to men and women - their needs - their aspirations - their social demands. As such, conservation is central to the domestic and international objectives of the American people."

—Cornelia Pinchot,
from 1949 speech La Wis Wis Forest Camp

"The greatest good for the greatest number..."

Pinchot's philosophy was that national forests should provide the "greatest good for the greatest number in the long run."

As Chief Forester, he greatly expanded the national forest system, which grew from 32 forest reserves in 1898 to 149 national forests in 1910, totaling 193 million acres.

> *"...among the many, many public officials who under my administration rendered literally invaluable service to the people of the United States, Gifford Pinchot on the whole, stood first."*
>
> *—President Theodore Roosevelt*

Pinchot was dismissed from his post in 1910 by President Taft, after a dispute with the Secretary of the Interior over coal leases in Alaska. After his dismissal, Pinchot remained active in the development of professional forestry and conservation issues.

Professional and Public Service of Gifford Pinchot from 1898–1936

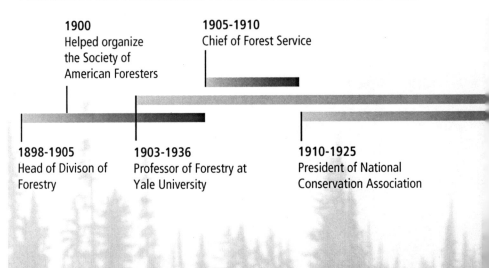

1900
Helped organize the Society of American Foresters

1905-1910
Chief of Forest Service

1898-1905
Head of Divison of Forestry

1903-1936
Professor of Forestry at Yale University

1910-1925
President of National Conservation Association

GIFFORD PINCHOT AND A GROUP OF FORESTERS

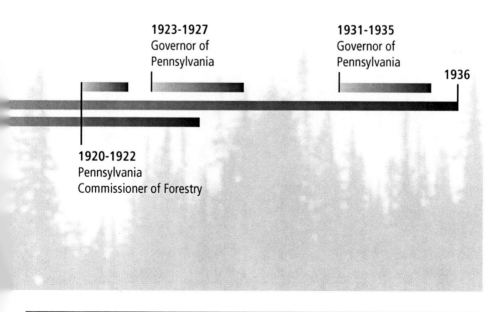

1923-1927
Governor of
Pennsylvania

1931-1935
Governor of
Pennsylvania

1936

1920-1922
Pennsylvania
Commissioner of Forestry

Early History

Tribal Use

Long before a word was ever written about this area, there were people here—people with a long and distinctive history. Some of that history survives in the oral traditions of tribal elders. More history is rediscovered each year through the work of archaeologists. As early as 7,000 years ago, people roamed these mountains, hunting and gathering an abundance of food resources. Their names have been lost to time, but the evidence they have left behind is beginning to tell their story, the earliest history of Gifford Pinchot National Forest.

FOUR CLACKAMA INDIANS, A PAINTING OF COLUMBIA RIVER INDIANS, PAUL KANE, 1847

At Layser Cave, high above the valley floor of the Cispus River, successive generations of these early people found shelter beginning around 5000 b.c. Similar early occupations have been found in the upper reaches of the Lewis River drainage, in the Trout Lake Creek drainage, and even along the crest of the Cascade Mountains. There is abundant evidence of later prehistoric occupation throughout the national forest, and in many places the archaeological record merges with oral history. Traditional camps used by Yakama people today have in many cases been used each summer over many centuries.

STONE TOOLS FROM STRATUM X, LAYSER CAVE, BROKEN AND LEFT BEHIND WITH REFUSE. THE SERRATED, LEAF-SHAPED PROJECTILE POINT ON THE LEFT IS TYPICAL OF EARLY SITES THROUGHOUT THE CASCADE RANGE.

NATIVE GEOGRAPHY LESSON

A small sampling of place names in the language of the Klickitat, Yakama, and Taidnapam people, with translations:

anawitash-nmi - "HUNGER PLACE" (NORTH FORK CISPUS RIVER)

kakya-lmi - "OF THE BIRD" (BIRD MOUNTAIN)

k'ashinu - "ELBOW" (DAVIS MOUNTAIN)

luluk-ash-waakuL - "RESEMBLES BREAST" (TWIN BUTTES)

shaxshax-nmi - "KINGFISHER PLACE" (TROUT LAKE)

xalia-xalia - "LITTLE BALSAMROOT" (LITTLE HUCKLEBERRY MOUNTAIN)

lma'ma - "OLD WOMAN" (LEMEI ROCK)

hool ho-olse - "MOUSE LAND" (CAVE CREEK)

JIM YOKE, SOURCE OF MANY TAIDNAPAM PLACE NAMES

Initial Exploration

When the first fur trappers and explorers visited this area in the early 1800s, they encountered people from several tribal groups. To the east were the Yakama and Klickitat. Along the Columbia River were the Wishram and Cascades people, and below them, the Multnomah. River valleys to the north were occupied by the Cowlitz and Taidnapam people.

All of these groups spent their summers in the mountains collecting a variety of foods and medicines. In August and September they would gather near the crest of the Cascade range, picking and drying huckleberries, trading, gambling, and socializing.

KLICKITAT HUCKLEBERRY BASKET

"There is no way through this space..."

In late May, 1830, a burly Irishman named John Work found himself soaked to the bone as he picked his way through dense brush and a maze of fallen trees. A clerk for the Hudson's Bay Company, Work was enroute to Fort Vancouver, led by Indian guides from The Dalles. Their trail took them west from what later became the town of Trout Lake into a mountainous region that was well known to local Indians, but *terra incognita* to the fur company men. John Work's account of the "troublesome" 1830 journey provides the first written description of lands that today make up part of Gifford Pinchot National Forest.

"May 22nd: The country we passed through this forenoon is dreadfully bad, a considerable portion of it burnt woods, immense trees fallen in every direction, and several deep ravines to cross, very steep for the horses to ascend and descend. Besides the woods are thicketty, and large fallen trees are so numerous that we could scarcely get any way found through it. There is no way through this space.

"May 30th: The men were completely drenched with rain all day yesterday and most of today, for though it did not rain today, the bushes are so charged with wet that a continual shower was falling as we passed through them. The road, exceedingly harassing all day, and men and horses much fatigued. It was past sunset when the men arrived, that were seeking the stray mare, and taking the horses out of the bog."

"May 31st: ...arrived at Fort Vancouver at 7 o'clock in the evening with 48 of our 50 horses, several of them nearly worn out... We are glad our difficult and troublesome journey is finished."

— *Journal of Hudson's Bay Company employee John Work, 1830*

GEORGE B. MCCLELLAN, 1826-1885

McClellan Expedition

In 1846 the boundary between the United States and Great Britain was set at the 49th parallel, and the Washington Territory was established by Congress in March of 1853. Isaac Stevens, who was appointed territorial governor and superintendent of Indian affairs, was to start negotiating treaties with the Indians, so that white settlement of the territory would not be hindered. Stevens was also to head a survey team to locate a railroad route across the Cascades to the Pacific. He appointed George McClellan to explore passes in the Cascades. Part of the purpose of McClellan's exploration was to assess Indian attitudes towards white settlement.

Leaving Fort Vancouver in July 1853, the expedition of 66 men and 173 horses and mules traveled along Indian trails to the Lewis River, eventually reaching the vicinity of Red Mountain and the Indian encampment of Chequoss, not far from the Big Lava Bed. From here they continued east, past Goose Lake, Peterson Prairie, and the White Salmon River, retracing the path taken by John Work, twenty-three years earlier. The journals of expedition members provide detailed observations of the country they passed through, along with a wealth of information about the native people they encountered.

Of his explorations in the Cascades, McClellan wrote: "I've just returned from the mountains, and a glorious old range it is—to look at; but awful to travel in."

But beauty is in the eye of the beholder:

> "The valley of the Cathlapoot'l [Lewis] above, and at our crossing, is utterly worthless for any purpose."
>
> —Captain George McClellan,
> GENERAL REPORT OF THE SURVEY OF THE CASCADES, 1854

From the journals of the expedition

> "Camp No. 14 - Chequoss. There are two ponds of water for the animals and a well for drinking purposes. Some 20 lodges of Indians in the vicinity. One died yesterday of the small pox—which disease is making great ravages among them."
>
> —George B. McClellan, JOURNAL, August 9, 1853

> "On the hills, there but partially covered with forests, we found, during our visit in the first week of August, a profusion of berries of several kinds, which the Indians were engaged in collecting. Among these was a huckleberry not before seen, with fruit nearly as large and finely flavored as a grape... Blue, purple, red, yellow and white flowers, in rich profusion, ornamented the surface; and the whole region looked more like a garden than a wild mountain summit, covered for nearly half the year with snow."
>
> —Dr. J. G. Cooper, REPORT ON THE BOTANY OF THE ROUTE, 1860

SKETCH MAP FROM THE 1853 JOURNAL OF DR. J. G. COOPER, NATURALIST WITH THE MCCLELLAN EXPEDITION, DEPICTING THEIR ROUTE FROM RED MOUNTAIN TO TROUT LAKE

On the morning of August 9, a rain having extinguished the burning of the forests below us, and cleared away the smoke which had for several days obscured the view, there was revealed to us a scene probably unsurpassed in magnificence by any in America. Five snowy peaks surrounded us, rising many thousand feet above our camp..."

—Dr. J. G. Cooper, REPORT ON THE BOTANY OF THE ROUTE, *1860*

Legend of the Lost Cannon

If you spend any time in the Mount Adams country you're bound to hear the legend of McClellan's lost cannon. The story is replete with sheepherders having seen the cannon in the 1940s, with a small tree growing through the bore. Although the legend of the cannon has taken on a life of its own, we can be fairly certain that it wasn't George McClellan who lost it. While assembling his expedition at Fort Vancouver in July of 1853, McClellan made a detailed list of the equipment and supplies that the party planned to carry. In his journal he described both the number and quality of transits, sextants, chronometers, levels, chains, and compasses that they had acquired. Of the 46 pack mules and 127 horses, he wrote "mules good, the horses indifferent." He wrote that they were "armed with U.S. rifles, Sharpe's rifles, and Colt's revolvers." But there is no mention of a cannon.

So, who lost it?

After McClellan, the second most likely loser of the cannon was Ulysses S. Grant, who between 1852 and 1853 served a stint at Fort Vancouver. But no one has ever come up with a good reason for Grant to have lost a cannon. His assignment while at the fort was quartermaster, and he left the Northwest several years before hostilities broke out between the Indians and the army.

Who really lost it?

One possibility is the cannon was lost by one of many parties of soldiers dispatched out of Fort Dalles during the "Indian Wars" of 1855-1858—men who were known to haul 200-pound "mountain howitzers" on mules, even while pursuing Indians through the mountains. In fact, Major Granville O. Haller reported "caching" a mountain howitzer (which was later recovered by the army) after an 1855 battle with Yakama Indians north and east of Mount Adams, apparently because the mule carrying it could no longer move forward. Could this be the origin of the legend of "McClellan's cannon?"

BENHAM HOMESTEAD, IRON CREEK AREA

The Public Domain

Under pressure from the United States government, leaders of the Yakama confederated bands and tribes signed the Treaty of 1855, ceding much of their traditional mountain territory to the United States and establishing the Yakama Indian Reservation. The Cowlitz refused to sign a treaty, and in 1864 Congress unilaterally extinguished their claims to the land. No treaty was ever made with the Cascades and Multnomah people in Washington, disease and warfare having taken their toll. The open "unclaimed," and unsettled lands of the southern Washington Cascade Range had officially come under the jurisdiction of the Department of the Interior, General Land Office.

Native people continued to use these lands, but encounters with others in the mountains became more common by the 1860s and 1870s. Early ascents of Mount St. Helens and Mount Adams included native guides. Prospectors searching for gold near Mount St. Helens used old Indian trails to reach their placer claims. The book *Gold Hunting in the Cascade Mountains*, written in 1861, describes a prospecting expedition along the headwaters of the Lewis River in 1860.

In the upper reaches of the Cowlitz River basin, local Indians led William Packwood to seams of "excellent bituminous coal," some of which were extensively developed in later years.

The Dark Divide and McCoy Creek areas are named for miners who searched these areas for gold in the 1880s.

Engineers from the Northern Pacific Railroad Company surveyed mountain passes along the crest of the Cascade Range south of Mount Rainier in 1867, 1878, and 1880. White Pass and Carlton Pass take their names from two of these men.

1891 HOMESTEAD OF ELIAS WIGAL, UPPER WIND RIVER VALLEY

Cowlitz Pass was initially assessed as "remarkably favorable" for a railroad, but ultimately never developed.

Homesteading

By the 1880s most land at low elevations had already been settled, and people began homesteading in more remote areas that would later be included in the forest reserves. The earliest such settlement was in the "Big Bottom" of the upper Cowlitz River valley, where William Joerk settled in 1883. An influx of families followed Joerk, most hailing from the Appalachian highlands. In the Little White Salmon River valley, at the far southern end of the forest, John Dark settled in 1885. In 1891, Elias Wigal settled in the Upper Wind River valley. Ole Peterson settled in the Lewis River valley, near the present town of Cougar, in 1893.

Many of these early homestead efforts were not successful. The Peters family built a log cabin and a barn at Peterson Prairie in the 1880s. Situated above 3,000 feet in elevation, the site of Peterson Prairie did not lend itself to raising cattle, and the family and their cows had to be rescued by settlers in Trout Lake their first winter. Their log cabin was later used as one of the earliest ranger stations.

Grazing

When Indians in this area first acquired horses in the mid-1700s, they brought them to the mountains to graze each summer. In August of 1878, a traveler named Francis Marion Streamer joined a group of Yakama Indians traveling to huckleberry fields on Mount Adams. When they reached their "Ollala Camp" on the northwest slopes of the mountain, Streamer noted in his journal: "There are now over one thousand ponies and nearly 200 Indians—and there will be as many more before the week…"

SHEEP GRAZING IN HELLROARING MEADOW ON THE SLOPES OF MOUNT ADAMS

By the mid-1880s, the grassy slopes of Mount Adams provided free summer feed for a different animal. Sheep were being trailed to the mountains from as far away as eastern Oregon. This was most likely a direct result of "the great conflagration of 1885," which burned thousands of acres of forest on the southern slopes of Mount Adams.

These first sheepherders included Charlie and Alexander McAllister, William Smith, Michael King, John O'Leary, and the Gotchen family. Estimates of the number of sheep grazing on Mount Adams before the turn of the century are staggering, ranging from 100,000 to 150,000 animals. At this time the range was unadministered, and hostilities broke out between Glenwood cattle ranchers and the sheepmen, both of whom were vying for the same range. The establishment of forest reserves and creation of separate sheep and cattle allotments administered by the early rangers eventually eased tensions between cattle ranchers and sheepmen.

"The pasturing of livestock on the forest reservations will not be interfered with so long as it appears that injury is not being done to the forest growth and the rights of others are not thereby jeopardized."

—Secretary of the Interior's rules,
June 30, 1897, article 13

NOTICE!

DEPARTMENT OF THE INTERIOR,

GENERAL LAND OFFICE,

WASHINGTON, D. C., APRIL 14, 1894.

Public notice is hereby given that these lands are set apart and reserved as a

FOREST RESERVATION,

BY PROCLAMATION OF THE PRESIDENT OF THE UNITED STATES, under authority of the act of Congress of March 3, 1891.

This reservation is made for the benefit of the adjoining communities, being created to maintain a permanent supply of water for irrigation and of wood for local use by a rational protection of the timber thereon.

ALL PERSONS ARE HEREBY WARNED

not to settle upon, occupy, or use any of these lands for agricultural, prospecting, mining, or other business purposes; nor to cut, remove, or use any of the timber, grass, or other natural product thereof, except under such regulations as may be hereafter prescribed.

No person shall start or kindle or allow to be started or kindled, ANY FIRE IN THE TIMBER, GRASS, OR UNDERGROWTH ON THESE LANDS, or commit any other waste thereon; and the DRIVING, FEEDING, GRAZING, PASTURING, OR HERDING OF CATTLE, SHEEP, OR OTHER LIVE STOCK WITHIN THIS RESERVATION, IS STRICTLY PROHIBITED.

Bona fide settlers having properly initiated their claims prior to the withdrawal of the lands for said reservation, and actual owners of lands within the reserve, may pass to and from their claims or property, but will not be allowed to occupy or use lands within the reservation outside of their claims, nor to use, damage, or destroy any timber or other natural product of such lands.

ANY PERSON VIOLATING THESE REGULATIONS WILL BE PROSECUTED FOR TRESPASS, and will be held responsible pecuniarily for any waste or damage, whether done intentionally or caused by neglect.

All law-abiding citizens are requested to report any cases of trespass upon said forest reserve that may come to their knowledge, and to assist in the prosecution of such trespasses.

APPROVED:

HOKE SMITH,
SECRETARY.

S. W. LAMOREUX,
COMMISSIONER.

G. F. ALLEN, FIRST PERMANENT SUPERVISOR, MOUNT RAINIER FOREST RESERVE

"This is my first inspection and report upon this reserve since the appointment of Supervisor G. F. Allen, September, 1902, and in the way of general remarks I respectfully report that no mistake was made in advancing Mr. Allen from the rank of Ranger to the important position as Supervisor. He is a careful and painstaking officer and works wholly in the interest of the reserve, and I can safely say that he is the most competent Supervisor I have had occasion to inspect."

—*D. B. Sheller,*
1905 report to Gifford Pinchot

Mount Rainier Forest Reserve

The Forest Reserve Act of 1891 gave the President authority to establish forest reservations from public domain lands. Department of the Interior field inspections in 1891 and 1892 led to recommendations for a reserve that would protect the forests around Mount Rainier. Thus, by proclamation of President Harrison, Pacific Forest Reserve was created in 1893.

Pacific Forest Reserve included much of what would later become Mount Rainier National Park. The southern boundary was drawn along township lines through the upper Cowlitz River valley. Regulations issued in 1894 were published in local newspapers and posted along the reserve boundaries. No one could "settle upon, occupy, or use any of these lands for agricultural, prospecting, mining, or other business purposes."

Gifford Pinchot came to the area in 1896 as a member of the special commission examining public timberlands in the West. His report made recommendations for a new, larger reserve that would include the Cascade Mountains south of Pacific Forest Reserve.

Incorporating the lands previously set aside as Pacific Forest Reserve, Mount Rainier Forest Reserve was created on February 22, 1897 by proclamation of President Grover Cleveland. The new 2,234,880—acre reserve was one of 13 added to the national system as a result of the special forest commission study.

PHOTOGRAPH FROM PLUMMER'S SURVEY DEMONSTRATES THE LARGE SIZE OF THE OLD GROWTH TIMBER IN THE FOREST RESERVE

The creation of the new forest reserves raised a storm of protest among western lumber, stock, and mining syndicates. Some members of Congress sought to impeach the President over the perceived outrage. Most of the opposition in the Pacific Northwest came from the Puget Sound region. Newspaper editorials were hostile, and the Washington state legislature appealed to Congress to cancel the reserves.

Opposition was strong in Skamania County, 80 percent of which lay within the reserve. Residents talked of combining with neighboring counties due to lack of an adequate tax base to support their own county. At the national level, however, public sentiment favored forest protection, and when the Senate passed an amendment to abolish the reserves in 1897, the measure was soundly defeated in the House.

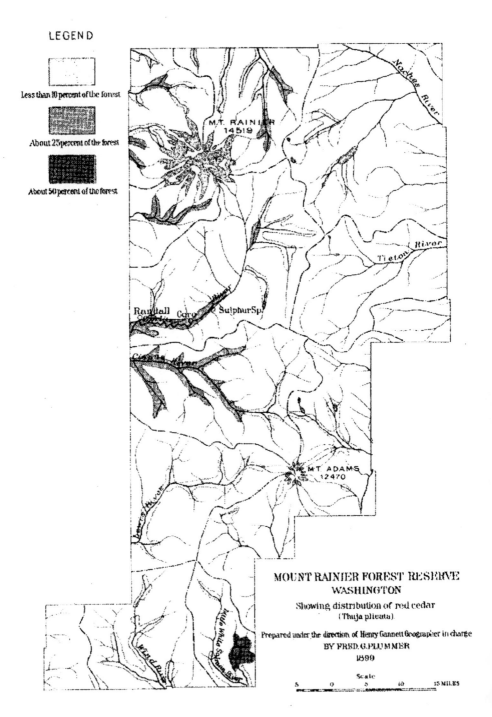

LEGEND

Less than 10 percent of the forest

About 25 percent of the forest

About 50 percent of the forest

M.T. RAINIER
14519

Naches River

Tieton River

Randall Coro. Sulphur Sp.

MT ADAMS
12470

Wind River

Little White Salmon River

MOUNT RAINIER FOREST RESERVE
WASHINGTON

Showing distribution of red cedar
(Thuja plicata)

Prepared under the direction of Henry Gannett Geographer in charge
BY FRED. G. PLUMMER
1899

Scale
5   0   5   10   15 MILES

MAP FROM PLUMMER'S REPORT SHOWING THE ORIGINAL BOUNDARIES OF THE MOUNT RAINIER FOREST RESERVE

"The routes of travel in the reserve are few. Most of the trails shown upon the map are hardly deserving of the name, but indicate blazed lines where better progress can be made than by taking a course through the timber and brush. The Indian's policy was to go only where his pony could take him, and the idea of cutting and logging out a trail was repugnant to him; therefore his lines of travel were along the sparsely timbered ridges, where feed was generally plenty, where game abounded, or where huckleberries grew. Later came the prospectors and sheepmen, and in some places they did considerable work."

—Fred G. Plummer,
Mount Rainier Forest Reserve, Washington, 1900

Plummer's Survey

The Forest Management Act ("Organic Act") of 1897 provided management provisions and funding for administration of the reserves, under the Department of the Interior, General Land Office. The Act redefined the purpose of the reserves as forest protection, watershed protection, and a source of timber supply for the nation.

In 1899, Fred Plummer, a U.S. Geological Survey engineer, completed the first comprehensive survey and mapping of Mount Rainier Forest Reserve. Plummer's report, published in 1900, includes the first detailed descriptions of forest types and conditions, hydrology, fire history, and grazing in the area that would eventually become Gifford Pinchot National Forest.

Mount St. Helens was initially left out of the reserve. The USGS recommended its addition, along with other lands in Clark, Skamania, and Cowlitz Counties. Their proposal was met by protests from railroad, timber, and commercial interests. Even Washington's governor opposed the plan. After the great Yacolt burn of 1902, however, there was little opposition, and in 1907 these areas were added to the reserve.

The First Rangers

From 1893 through 1897 administration of the forest reserves fell to a small corps of deputy United States marshals and General Land Office special agents. Overwhelmed by other duties, they could in no way serve as a protective force. It was not until 1898 that the General Land Office received authority and funding to hire rangers for this purpose. In the summer of that year, Frank Gates, a settler

A. B. CONRAD, GENERAL LAND OFFICE RANGER

living in the Cowlitz River valley above Randle, became the first ranger hired on Mount Rainier Forest Reserve. Gates used his homestead as headquarters and had nearly all the forest lands in eastern Lewis County as his district. He served two or three seasons before leaving the area.

In 1900, the General Land Office appointed George McCoy to the position of supervisor of the reserve. Little is known about McCoy, who maintained reserve headquarters in Napavine, and who, like the two or three rangers he hired, was a seasonal employee.

During the following year, the General Land Office appointed Dave Sheller, a Tacoma politician, as superintendent to oversee administration of the three forest reserves in the state of Washington.

In 1902, Sheller hired three new forest rangers for Mount Rainier Forest Reserve. The first of these was Grenville F. Allen. Trained as an engineer at Yale, G. F. Allen had previously worked for the U. S. Geological Survey and on logging operations in the forests near Mount Rainier. Allen was initially offered the position of supervisor of the forest reserve, but turned it down in order to first gain a season of work experience as a ranger.

Allen spent much of his first season traveling around the reserve, working with Horace Wetherell and John Schmitz, the other new rangers. Wetherell, a Carson area homesteader, was the first forest ranger on the southern end of the reserve. Schmitz, too, was a homesteader, living at Sulphur Springs, near present-day Packwood. He filled the vacancy left by Frank Gates in the Cowlitz Valley.

JOHN SCHMITZ, GENERAL LAND OFFICE RANGER 1902-1905 IN COWLITZ VALLEY

G. F. Allen became the first full-time supervisor of the forest reserve in the fall of 1902. In the following year, he added Charles E. Randle and W. W. Cryder to the ranger force. Randle was the son of a pioneering family for whom the town of Randle was named. Summer work consisted of posting boundary notices and fire warnings, surveying and marking the boundaries of homestead claims, investigating timber trespass, trail improvement and construction, grazing inspections, and fire patrols. Rangers went all over the reserve to assist each other with work projects.

Other rangers appointed to Mount Rainier Forest Reserve under the General Land Office administration included Alfred B. Conrad and William McCullough, assigned in 1904 to cover the Nisqually and Carbon River Districts. Until 1906, their duties also included Mount Rainier National Park. Homer Ross was hired in 1904. He worked from his home in Glenwood, dealing mostly with grazing issues. Elias J. Wigal replaced Horace Wetherell as ranger in the Wind River valley in 1904.

"I went on duty as a Forest Ranger on the Rainier Forest [Reserve] on July 2, 1902. Grenville F. Allen was appointed Ranger about the same time... In addition to fire protection work, we posted boundary notices and fire warnings and kept the trails open. Mr. Allen was soon appointed supervisor, leaving me as the only Ranger in that particular district."

—John M. Schmitz, 1949 memoir

"In the spring of 1904... I decided to try and get a job for the summer as a range rider. I made application to Mr. G. F. Allen, who was Supervisor of the Rainier Forest Reserve. In due time I was hired at $60.00 per month for July, August and September of that

year. I furnished two saddle horses, one pack horse, and as the Swede said, 'Ate myself'. I liked the work and liked the men I came in contact with, and, also, enjoyed wearing that big, round nickel-plated badge."

—Homer Ross, 1940 letter to Gifford Pinchot

"Horace Wetherell received his appointment as Forest Ranger June 1, 1902 and was assigned to the Wind River Valley and adjoining territory. No limits were placed on the territory he was expected to cover. His salary was $60.00 per month and he was required to furnish a horse, saddle and such other equipment as he needed to carry on his work.

There were no buildings, no trails, phone lines or any other improvements. His job was to patrol the forest, put out all fires and to prevent timber theft.

When Mr. Wetherell told me this, I made the remark that it was quite a job for one man to undertake. He

FRITZ SETHE, ASSISTANT FOREST RANGER AT HEMLOCK

RANGERS CLYDE WETHEREALL AND HARVEY LICKEL CAMP AT RACE TRACK, 1911

replied that he was eighty-three years old and never during that time had he ever had a harder or more disagreeable job than as a Forest Ranger."

—Ross Shepeard
from HISTORY NOTES ON WIND RIVER DISTRICT, *January 24, 1938*

Pinchot Takes Charge

In the spring of 1905 Congress transferred the forest reserves from the Department of the Interior to the Department of Agriculture, and in July of 1905 the Bureau of Forestry was renamed the U.S. Forest Service.

Gifford Pinchot was appointed the first chief forester for the newly created Forest Service, having sought the transfers of the reserves from the time he was appointed chief forester of the Division of Forestry in the U.S. Department of Agriculture in 1898. Pinchot drafted instructions on managing the reserves, stating that "All of the resources of the forest reserves are for use... under such restrictions only as will insure the permanence of these resources." These regulations were first published in 1905 as *The Use Book*.

In 1907 the federal forest reserves were renamed national forests, in order to correct the impression that they were withdrawn from use. In 1908, Rainier National Forest was split into Rainier National Forest on the north and Columbia National Forest on the south.

"All of us took many a ride or walk all day through rain, snow or whatever weather without a thought of complaint, just taking it as a matter of duty. We received no traveling expenses and had to furnish our own equipment, even tools for trail work. Sometimes we would have to borrow a saw from some settler. We had no improvement fund—the Rangers

EILERT SKAAR AT TWIN BUTTES RANGER STATION, 1911

did everything and all for $60 a month, although we were raised to $75 a month in 1903. But it wasn't so bad, except when we had to replace a horse. Our board, including hay for a horse, was about 75 cents a day, so we got by and rather enjoyed the work."

—*John M. Schmitz, 1949 memoir*

Beginning in 1905, the Forest Service required applicants for forest ranger positions to take practical written and field examinations to determine their knowledge of basic ranching and livestock, forest conditions, lumbering, surveying, mapping, cabin construction, and so on. The field examination required the applicant to demonstrate practical skills, such as how to saddle a horse and ride at a trot and gallop, pack a horse or mule, tie a diamond hitch, accurately pace the distance around a measured course and compute the area in acres, and take bearings with a compass and follow a straight line.

H.O. STABLER, COLUMBIA NATIONAL FOREST SUPERVISOR, 1908-1913

In early years the applicants were also required to demonstrate accuracy with firearms. The applicants were not furnished with equipment, horses, or pack animals—they were required to provide them for the test and for the job, at their own expense.

"The Rangers are the men who carry out the work on the ground... The Ranger must be able to take care of himself and his horses under very trying conditions; build trails and cabins; ride all day and all night; pack, shoot, and fight fire without losing his head. He must know a good deal about the timber of the country, and how to estimate it; he must be familiar with lumbering and the sawmill business, the handling of live stock, mining, and the land laws. All this requires a very vigorous constitution. It means the hardest kind of physical work from beginning to end."

"The life a man has led, what is his actual training and experience in rough outdoor work in the West, counts for more than anything else. Lumbermen, stockmen, cowboys, miners, and the like are the kind wanted."

—*Gifford Pinchot,* THE USE OF THE NATIONAL FORESTS, *1907*

"I was assigned the job of surveying and mapping all the sites that might be needed for administrative purposes on the east slopes of the Rainier Forest from the Columbia River to the Goat Rocks. I knew very little about surveying and mapping, but had studied the use of the compass and worked some with men who were willing to teach me... They sent me a compass, chain and a scribe, but no one to carry the other end of the chain. I met that situation by taking my wife with me. We had been married then about 2 years and she, being the daughter of a cattleman, was as much at home if not more so in the mountains than I. We traveled through the mountains together most of that summer, surveying and mapping administrative sites when not counting sheep or fighting forest fires."

—*Homer Ross, 1940 letter to Gifford Pinchot*

Creation of Columbia National Forest

Columbia National Forest was established by Executive Order of President Theodore Roosevelt on July 1, 1908, created from the southern districts of Rainier National Forest. The headquarters was initially located in Portland, Oregon. In 1927, it was moved to Vancouver, Washington.

"The executive force of the Columbia National Forest is made up of men who are particularly well fitted for the various lines of work in which they are engaged. Each man on this Forest seems to take a thorough interest in his work, and shows a particular loyalty to the Forest Service. The Rangers and Guards are an energetic, enthusiastic lot of men who are willing at all times to perform their duties under the most severe and trying conditions."

—*J. B. Knapp, 1909 inspection report*

"Only a small amount of improvement work had been done on this Forest before its separation from the Rainier. There were only one or two Ranger Station cabins, no pastures and no improved trails. At the present time there are within the Forest 39 miles of wagon road and 329 miles of improved old and new trails, 28 miles of private telephone lines, 6 miles of Forest Service telephone lines, 8 Ranger cabins and 7 pasture fences."

—*Arthur R. Wilcox, 1911 report*

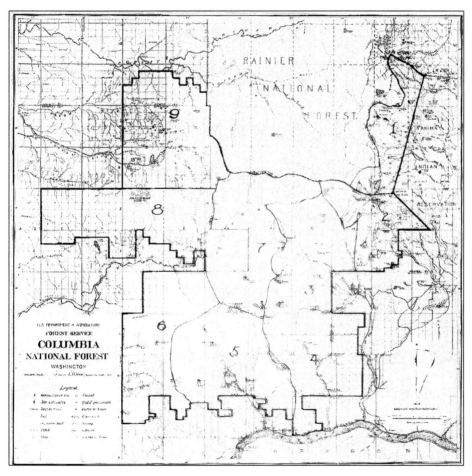

FIRST MAP OF THE COLUMBIA NATIONAL FOREST, 1909

BECK BUILDING, PORTLAND, OREGON. FIRST HEADQUARTERS OF THE COLUMBIA NATIONAL FOREST

Forest Organization in 1909

SUPERVISOR'S OFFICE - (PORTLAND)
H. O. STABLER, FOREST SUPERVISOR
ARTHUR R. WILCOX, FOREST ASSISTANT
JULIA M. BOARDMAN, CLERK

DISTRICT 1 - (GLENWOOD)
HOMER ROSS, FOREST RANGER
C. W. COMBS, FOREST GUARD

DISTRICT 2 - (GULER)
O. W. PIERCE, FOREST GUARD

DISTRICT 3 - (PETERSON PRAIRIE R. S.)
HARRY DEVOE, FOREST GUARD

DISTRICT 4 - (OKLAHOMA R. S.)
FRANK MILLER, FOREST GUARD
DONALD CAMPBELL, FOREST GUARD

DISTRICT 5 - (HEMLOCK R.S.)
ELIAS J. WIGAL, DEPUTY FOREST RANGER
W. F. JEBE, SCALER

DISTRICT 6 - (DOLE)
CHARLES FREUDENBURG, FOREST GUARD

DISTRICT 7 - (UPPER LEWIS RIVER)
MAC WRIGHT, FOREST GUARD

DISTRICT 8 - (COUGAR)
FRITZ SETHE, FOREST GUARD

DISTRICT 9 - (SPIRIT LAKE)
ERASMUS B. ROBERTSON, FOREST GUARD

RANGER E. J. WIGAL BUILT THE FIRST RANGER STATION AT HEMLOCK IN 1906. HIS DIARY (SEE EXCERPTS) PROVIDES A DETAILED RECORD OF A RANGER'S DUTIES.

A Closer Look at the Early Districts

Hemlock/Wind Ranger District

The ranger in charge of Wind River between 1904 and 1911 was Elias J. Wigal, who homesteaded in the Wind River Valley in 1891. Wigal initially worked out of his home, which was located between Hemlock and Carson, but by 1906 he had constructed the first district office, on the south side of Trout Creek, close to Wind River Lumber Company's Camp 3. One of Wigal's duties was to administer the timber sales sold to Wind River Lumber Company, the first of which was in May of 1906.

This one-room cabin was the first ranger station constructed on the reserve. It was designated Hemlock Ranger Station, due to the large number of hemlock trees in the vicinity.

In 1908 Wigal built a second ranger station at Hemlock, next to the first. This cabin was two stories high and constructed entirely of hewn cedar logs, four inches thick and from fourteen-inches to twenty-six-inches wide. The house was covered with split and shaved shingles and painted green. The "green house," as it was called, served both as a headquarters for the ranger in charge of the Wind River timber sales and as living quarters for Forest Service scalers.

Several ranger stations were established on the Wind River District to aid in administration, including Race Track, Trapper Creek, Howe, Trout Creek, Summit Springs, McClellan Meadows, and Panther Creek Ranger Stations.

Excerpts from Ranger E. J. Wigal's diary, 1909

Camp Suplies
May 1   1909
1 Sack flower   .75
6 cans Tomatoes   60
5 corn   50
20 lb beans   1.00
1 box apples   1.25
1 can baking Powder   .50
                      4.60

Meyer Kelley Co   .50

S J Smith an Son $18.00
                 $29.10
Stater natzel   4 00
                 27.10

June 11
wash bord

July 1   1909
8 am left Hemlock
Station went up the
rock Creek trail to
finish locating it up
the mt went over to the
Stevenson trail went to
camp wrote letters got
a Phone message from
Little white Salmon that
there was a fire there left
Hemlock camped at home
7 Pm

October 19   1909
7 am been raining
helping the black Smith
draw out grubbing hoes
I and Pierce ground
hoes and axes camped
5 Pm

October 20
got packs togather
left Hemlock went
to camp one with
mr Pearce to Start
out on the rout of
the new trail to
the race track
raining too hard
to go out in the
brush Staied at
camp one

Elias Wigal resigned in 1911, and Fritz Sethe served as ranger from 1911 to 1915. Sethe was seriously injured in 1915 while clearing land for the Wind River Nursery, and left the forest service. He was replaced by Eilert Skaar, and then George Williams, who, like Sethe, began his career as a ranger in the Lewis River country. In an interview in the 1940s, Williams recalled that by 1917 college men were beginning to replace the "rough and ready ranger." He decided it was time to look for a new job. Later rangers at Wind River included Axel Erickson, Clifford Welty, James Huffman, Ross Shepeard, Carlos Brown, J. H. Wood, William Johnson, and Don Fechtner.

REGION SIX PERSONNEL TRAINING STATION (HODGSON-LINDBERG TRAINING CENTER)

A Training Center for Rangers

In 1931 Wind River was chosen as the location of a ranger training school, with Allen Hodgson as director. During the first few years the rangers camped in tents, and most instruction took place outdoors. In 1936 plans were finalized for the construction of a training center and dormitory, for use as a regional meeting and training facility. Completed in 1937, the Region Six Personnel Training Station served for decades as the primary training facility in the region. The facility is stil in use and listed on the national register of historic places.

Wind River Lumber Company

Wind River Lumber Company began operations around 1900 in the Wind River valley. During this time the only way to feasibly transport logs from the upper valley was to float them down the Wind River to the Columbia River, through the use of splash dams. Logs were contained in ponds behind the dams and released in large quantities through the floodgates. Wind River Lumber Company operated three of these splash dams on the forest reserve: one on the Wind River, one on Trout Creek, and another on Panther Creek.

In 1906, the lumber company was awarded one of the first timber sales on national forest lands. This sale cut a total of 14,626,250 board feet in the Wind River valley, at a total value of $12,921.89.

Loggers used steam-powered donkey engines to skid logs to landings via a haulback line. This line could also be used to winch the donkey through the woods.

RANGER FRITZ SETHE (CENTER) INSPECTS WIND RIVER LUMBER COMPANY STEAM DONKEY YARDING

The company began railroad logging operations in 1913, which allowed it access to timber in the upper reaches of the Wind River. The first two miles of standard gauge railroad were completed in 1913, and by 1925 the company had built more than 30 miles of main railroad line and numerous spurs. Logs were dumped in the river at Camp 1, and floated to the Columbia.

A forest fire south of Falls Creek burned 4.5 million board feet of felled and bucked logs in 1925, resulting in the lumber company's bankruptcy. Company lands were sold, and one of these parcels eventually became part of the Wind River administrative site.

"The logging foreman informed me that the fire last July was caused by a defective spark arrester on a locomotive. Forest officers in charge of sales have no more important supervisory duty than to see that spark arresters are constantly in good condition."

—*F. E. Ames, Assistant District Forester,* MEMORANDUM OF INSPECTION, *1915*

SPLASH DAM ON TROUT CREEK, ca. 1910

PLOWING NURSERY FIELD, 1910

Wind River Nursery

Plans were drawn up in November, 1909 for the Wind River Nursery, located at the site of Hemlock Ranger Station. This area had been burned in the Yacolt fire of 1902, and was partly logged in a timber sale purchased by Wind River Lumber Company in May, 1906.

The nursery's primary purpose was to grow trees to reforest the Bull Run watershed, the source of the city of Portland's water supply. Approximately 8,000 acres of this watershed had burned in the 1890s. The secondary purpose of the nursery was to reforest other large burns, as a future financial investment in timber production.

Forest Ranger E. J. Wigal hired three men to work on clearing the five-acre tract. This required blasting stumps with powder, clearing away the stumps, filling the holes left behind, plowing and replowing the ground, burning or removing the remaining roots and debris, and leveling the land by means of scraper, shovels, harrow, and float.

By April, 1910, Assistant Forest Ranger Charles Miner had been hired and placed in charge.

The first seed beds were installed in 1910, and the five acres were planted with black walnut, shagbark hickory, pignut, white ash, mulberry, box elder, black cherry, black locust, red oak, Scotch pine, European larch, maritime pine, western white pine, Douglas-fir, noble fir, red cedar, and Norway spruce.

COVERED SEED BEDS IN NURSERY, 1910

DOUGLAS-FIR AND WESTERN WHITE PINE WERE THE PRINCIPAL TREE SPECIES GROWN, BUT EXPERIMENTAL PLANTINGS OF HARDWOODS WERE CONDUCTED FOR THE FIRST TWO YEARS. THE HARDWOODS WERE SOWN BY HAND IN ROWS, WITH FURROWS OPENED BY MEANS OF A CULTIVATOR

SOWING SEEDS IN SEED BEDS

TRANSPLANTING WITH A MICHIGAN BOARD

"Work at the Wind River Nursery will start next week. You should take the 8:20 morning train on the North Bank Railroad Monday, April 7, and go to Carson, Washington. You will probably have to walk to the nursery, which is twelve miles from Carson. The Government team will probably be in town and can take your bed roll, if the wagon is not overloaded."

—Arthur Wilcox, Acting Forest Supervisor,
letter to seasonal nursery workers, 1913

The first seedlings were shipped in 1911, and in that year Miner was replaced by Arthur Wilcox. At this time all the rangers and guards on the forest were required to work on the nursery at certain times of the year, particularly during the months of March, April, and November.

In 1912 all seedlings and transplants were dug with a long-handled spade, with one man lifting and one man digging. A "Michigan" planting board was used for transplanting seedlings. The board consisted of a one-inch-by-six-inch board, seven feet long, with narrow slots sawed into one-quarter-inch holes bored one-quarter-inch from the edge of the board and placed according to the desired spacing. It was placed over a trench, the seedlings placed in the holes, and the trench filled as the board was lifted.

William F. Will took charge of nursery operations in 1920, and remained until his retirement in 1944. Will was responsible for many innovations at the nursery.

By 1925, fourteen-acres had been cleared for nursery use. Seeds were still broadcast in four-foot-by-twelve-foot frames. Seedlings were lifted with the root pruner, pulled by two horses. Cover crops of oats and vetch were planted and plowed under to provide nutrients to the soil.

A new Cletrac tractor was purchased in 1927 for nursery use, equipped with a hoisting drum for operating the tree lifter. This replaced the nursery's horse team, which was sold for $140.

Forrest Deffenbacher became Wind River Nursery's director in 1946. Under his direction the nursery expanded rapidly and became more mechanized. The old four-foot-by-twelve-foot seed bed boxes were removed and long rows of seedbeds were sown with a seed drill attached to a tractor, referred to as the Wind River seeder. Machine sowing allowed six to seven million seeds to be sown in a day. A tractor cultivator was

WIND RIVER ARBORETUM

used for weeding. Deffenbacher designed and built tables with moving belts for grading the seedlings. Women formed an integral part of the nursery workforce.

Wind River Nursery closed in 1997, after eighty-eight years in operation. Forest nursery practices throughout the West are founded on pioneering research conducted at this nursery.

Wind River Experiment Station

In May of 1912, C. R. Tillotson was detailed from the Washington office to direct experimental work at Wind River Nursery. The decision was made to locate an experiment station in conjunction with the nursery, since nursery practice and planting techniques were important areas of research. During that first season a laboratory was constructed, which also served as a residence for the employees, along with a greenhouse for seed tests.

Early experimental work was aimed primarily at improvements in nursery practice, such as sowing, shading, mulching, irrigating, and planting. A Douglas-fir seed source study was initiated, along with several other studies.

The first trees were officially planted for the Wind River arboretum in 1912, making it one of the oldest arboretums in the Northwest. The original purpose was to test the suitability of non-native species for forest planting in the Pacific Northwest.

Between 1912 and 1913, the experimental work was part of nursery operations. In 1913, Wind River Experiment Station was officially established, with J. V. Hoffman as director.

When the Pacific Northwest Forest Experiment Station was formed in Portland in 1924, the Wind River station was redesignated as a fieldwork center. Research activities ebbed during World War II, but expanded after the war, with an emphasis on timber harvest and regeneration problems. By the late 1950s the role of the Wind River station as a primary research location had declined, and since that time studies have been administered from the Forestry Sciences Laboratories in Olympia and Corvallis.

Silvicultural concepts, cutting practices, reforestation methods, and genetic studies developed at Wind River Experiment Station form the basis for modern forestry practices.

"It is planned to inaugurate a set of intensive experiments on and in the vicinity of the Wind River Nursery with a view towards the possible establishment of a forest experiment station there at a later date... It will be necessary to devote a part of the nursery to experimental use."

—*Assistant Regional Forester Judd, 1912 memo*
to Forest Supervisor H. O. Stabler

WIND RIVER EXPERIMENT STATION, 1917, WITH NURSERY FIELD IN FOREGROUND

Guler/Mount Adams Ranger District

"The spring of 1904 I was sent to the Mt. Adams district to count the sheep entering the forest. It was the first time I had done such work and after standing there and counting 10,000 head through the chute, I didn't know much about where I was at, so I took the herders' word for the rest of them."

— *John M. Schmitz, 1949 memoir*

Homer Ross may have been the earliest ranger to work on Mount Adams Ranger District. Ross, who began his career with the forest reserves as a guard in 1904, made his home in Glenwood, which served as his headquarters.

In 1909 the forest was divided into as many as nine "districts," with several ranger stations in what later became Mount Adams Ranger District. These stations were strategically located across the forest, often within a day's ride of each other. Some, such as Ice Cave, Cultus Creek, Wicky Creek, and Goose Lake, merely served as base camps where water and forage were available. Others served as "headquarters" for the early "districts."

The earliest "headquarters" was probably Peterson Prairie, where the abandoned homestead cabin of the Peters family was used as a ranger station as early as 1907. Harrison DeVoe was forest guard stationed at Peterson in 1909.

"During the past summer Forest Guard DeVoe patrolled all the country south, east and west of Mt. Adams, in all about 85,000 acres, and with such a large area to look after it is obvious no more than 40 or 50% of the area was patrolled daily."

—H. O. Stabler, 1910 Fire Report

The first ranger station cabin constructed by the forest service on Mount Adams Ranger District was Gotchen Creek Ranger Station, built as summer headquarters in 1909. The cabin was connected by wagon road to Glenwood, where Forest Ranger Homer Ross maintained district headquarters in his home. Almost all of the sheep entering the forest did so by way of the road past Gotchen Creek, where they could easily be counted by the ranger stationed there.

Assistant Ranger L. E. Lucas, with headquarters at Guler in 1908, is the first ranger on record to be stationed in the town that we now call Trout Lake. It is likely that Lucas, along with Orville W. Pierce in 1909 and 1910, worked from their homes in Guler, since a ranger station headquarters wasn't established there until 1917.

FOREST GUARD HARVEY LICKEL BORROWED LUMBER, WINDOWS, AND DOOR FRAMES FROM THREE ABANDONED HOMESTEAD CABINS TO CONSTRUCT OKLAHOMA RANGER STATION IN 1910. THESE HOMESTEADS REPRESENTED THE LAST VESTIGES OF THE "OKLAHOMA BOOMERS" WHO ATTEMPTED TO SETTLE THE LITTLE WHITE SALMON VALLEY IN THE 1890S. ALTHOUGH NOT CONSIDERED "HEADQUARTERS," SMALL PATROL CABINS WERE ALSO BUILT AT DEAD HORSE, OLLALIE, SOUTH PRAIRIE, MORRISON CREEK, AND TWIN BUTTES BY 1910.

ORIN PEARSON (LEFT) AND RANGER HARVEY WELTY (SECOND FROM RIGHT) AT GULER RANGER STATION

Harvey Lickel, the ranger stationed at Guler between 1912 and 1918, was probably responsible for constructing the first district ranger's headquarters at Guler, a combination office/residence that still stands at Mount Adams Ranger Station.

Lickel's successor, Jesse Mann, built a barn at the ranger station in 1920. The six men that assisted him represented the entire permanent work force of Columbia National Forest in 1920.

Harvey Welty served as district ranger between 1923 and 1933.

"On July 31, Mrs. Welty and myself finished a 25-day field trip, visiting the following places: Peterson, Little Huckleberry, Willard, Race Track, Goose Lake, Lost and Found Fire (not visiting on fire working), Quartz Creek ridge, Sleeping Beauty Way, Twin Buttes Lookout, Spencer Butte, Pepper Creek Trail, Luginbuhl and Berney sheep allotments, Twin Buttes road camp."

—*Harvey Welty, Mt. Adams District Ranger,* THE COLUMBIA RECORD, *1926*

"The District Ranger has been traveling so fast on his trips around the mountain with his pack string that we've almost given up hopes of catching him."

—*editorial comment,* THE COLUMBIA RECORD, *1926*

"Guler Barn - Built in fall of 1920. The building limitation permitted only the purchase

GULER BARN UNDER CONSTRUCTION

of the material, with enough left over to hire Carl Pearson a short time. So, we all got together and did the work. Jess Mann, Axel Erickson, Welty Bros., Farnam, Supervisor Brundage, and I. Don't remember any others. It took about three weeks. We bached as there wasn't money for meals at hotel. Work finished about Thanksgiving, and we had Thanksgiving dinner at Mann's. The mill was slow in getting out lumber, so Jess Mann went up and ran the sawmill. This barn was quite a project at the time, and Jess wanted it just right. It was 30' x 60', 34' high, with bank roof to allow maximum storage for loose hay, which the rangers bought in the field before it was harvested."

—Harry White, former Deputy Forest Supervisor, comments for the COLUMBIA HISTORICAL RECORD, *1949*

Karl C. "K. C." Langfield, who served as district ranger at Mount Adams for 23 years, was a legend of sorts.

After being chewed out by Langfield for leaving the station one day during fire season to help his neighbors pitch hay, a young forester griped that K. C. was nothing but a "Pine tree shield with feet on it." Most people agreed that K. C. would have considered that a compliment. Employees joked that he was such a company man, they carried him on the property records at the Regional Office. He was totally dedicated to the Forest Service. In 1954 he was awarded the Superior Service Award from the Department of Agriculture, in recognition of his effective leadership and his ability to train young men.

"In your many years of service, you have been a splendid representative of our organization and one whose record may well be a challenge to meet by the men you have so ably trained in your profession."

—Secretary of Agriculture Ezra Taft Benson, 1956 letter to K. C. Langfield

HEAD COOK, DISHWASHER, AND RANGER, K. C. LANGFIELD (LEFT) IN INDIAN HEAVEN AREA

LANGFIELD AND STAFF CROSSING THE LEWIS RIVER NEAR ISLAND SHELTER

LANGFIELD (LEFT) AND STAFF RETRIEVE STOCK FROM WINTER PASTURE IN KLICKITAT

SPIRIT LAKE AND MOUNT ST. HELENS

Spirit Lake Ranger District

Indian people living near Mount St. Helens told of a lake where the salmon could not be taken because they were the spirits of dead warriors. Fearsome creatures were said to live around the lake, discouraging native hunters. The ancient stories did not prevent prospectors from exploring the Spirit Lake basin in their quest for gold and silver. Mineral-bearing rock was found in 1891, and the following year prospectors flocked to the area to stake claims. Tunnels were opened, cabins built, and by 1900 the wagon road from Castle Rock extended up the Toutle River to the shores of Spirit Lake.

Mining claim development was in full swing during the early years of Mount Rainier Forest Reserve. With forest protection a concern, a forest guard was stationed at Spirit Lake during the summer, beginning in 1907. Herbert L. Hurd of Centralia, was the first, reportedly "sent out by Gifford Pinchot." In 1908, Edgar B. Johnston held the job. During that year the St. Helens Ore, Milling, and Power Company was at work building a flume line at Spirit Lake. One of the men employed in the construction was 25-year-old Erasmus E. Robertson. An enthusiastic and conscientious worker, Robertson took the forest guard job from 1909 through 1912, and again in 1915 and 1916. An abandoned homestead cabin, described as "hardly habitable," was used as the first ranger station at Spirit Lake.

Robertson was joined in 1911 by George Williams, the first full-time district ranger. Like Robertson, Williams had also worked for a mining company at Spirit Lake. In 1910, Williams entered the forest service as ranger with headquarters at Toutle Ranger Station, which he built in that year. A new guard station was also built at Spirit Lake, which did not become the district headquarters until

1913. Williams' salary was $100 a month and he was required to furnish and feed three horses. His fire patrol district included Green River, Spirit Lake, Meta Lake, Goat Marsh, Butte Camp, and the Lewis River. In 1911 he carried out classification surveys throughout the forest with W. G. Hastings, spending thirty days on foot and covering 300 miles. Besides fire patrols, Spirit Lake guard and ranger duties involved trail work, mineral claim inspections, boundary surveys, and the examination of forest homestead claims.

In 1909 the Lewis River country was administered by Forest Guard Fritz Sethe, whose headquarters were at Cougar. Sethe spent most of his time carrying out trail work and fire patrols. Lewis River Ranger Station was established sometime before 1910 near the homestead of Ole Peterson, about three miles east of the community

GEORGE WILLIAMS MAKES NOTES DURING A HOMESTEAD INSPECTION, 1910

of Cougar. Lewis River Ranger Station was used by rangers, guards, and packers traveling to the Lewis River area from the west side. In 1931 a new guard station was built, along with a garage and barn.

Over the years, Spirit Lake became a popular summer getaway. Rangers Cliff Welty, Jim Huffman, Monty Mapes, Al Wang, Peter Wyss, Harvey Welty, and Richard Tubman and saw the complete decline of mineral development and a steady increase in recreation use during their time in service at Spirit Lake.

In 1948, Lewis River Ranger District was officially created as a separate district because of the extensive timber sale development planned for the area. Heath V. Hall was the first district ranger, with summer headquarters at Lewis River Guard Station and winter headquarters in the Post Office building at Kelso.

PORTAL OF THE SWEDEN MINE, LARGEST IN THE SPIRIT LAKE BASIN, ca. 1905

St. Helens Mining District: A field of disappointments

Mineral-bearing rocks were discovered in the Spirit Lake basin in 1891. Prospectors flocked to the area, which became known as St. Helens Mining District. More than 400 claims were filed on gold, copper, and silver deposits between 1892 and 1911. Robert Lange established one of the first mines at Spirit Lake and is said to have dug one hundred thousand tons of ore by 1910.

Claim development was usually financed through sales of stock. Lange found investors for his mining company in Europe. Another company had financial ties to a Milwaukee newspaper. Mount St. Helens Consolidated Mining Company, under direction of Dr. Henry Coe, even boasted Theodore Roosevelt as a stockholder. Coe's company established a

ADVERTISEMENT FOR TUM TUM MINES

camp employing 40 men at the Sweden and Norway Mines near Spirit Lake, reportedly spending $700,000 to sink a tunnel 2,800 feet into the side of the mountain. The Sweden Mine was the only claim in the entire district to produce ore for smelting. In 1905, some thirteen tons were barged across Spirit Lake and transported by wagon to Castle Rock, then shipped to a Portland smelter.

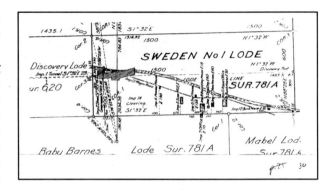

MINING CLAIM PLAT - NORWAY/SWEDEN MINES

Claim development in the district peaked around 1904-1908, but mineral quality was not high enough to offset transportation costs. With no prospect of road or rail access, most claims were abandoned within a few years.

"The St. Helens district is essentially a copper district, as is shown by the assays of ores coming therefrom, excepting a few ledges in the northern part of the zone, which shows decidedly good gold value."

—Harvey Bailey, MINING WORLD, V. 22, NO. 22, *1905*

Recreation at Spirit Lake

Mining promoter Henry Coe undoubtedly saw the potential for Spirit Lake as a summer getaway. By 1904, he had built two cabins on a mineral claim at Harmony Point on the shores of Spirit Lake and was entertaining guests from Portland. Coe's shoreline development would in later years become a colony of upscale summer homes surrounding Harmony Falls Lodge.

MINERS AT THE ENTRANCE TO THE PORTLAND MINE, 1904

A GROUP ASCENT OF MOUNT ST. HELENS

SPIRIT LAKE LODGE, BUILT BY PORTLAND YMCA IN 1913

THE ST. HELENS FOREST SERVICE PATROL BOAT ON SPIRIT LAKE, 1938

A primitive YMCA camp for boys was established at the lake in 1909, marking the beginning of organizational summer camps at the lake. In 1911 the Portland YMCA received a special use permit to develop a permanent camp at the south end of the lake. Spirit Lake Lodge, built in 1913, became a center of activity at the camp. Cabins were added in the early 1920s, and in 1928 a massive second lodge was built.

The Forest Service established a public campground at Spirit Lake. The area gained in popularity in the 1920s and 1930s. Summer visitors came for camping, picnicking, boating, swimming, fishing, hiking, horseback riding, berry picking, and hunting.

Some came to climb Mount St. Helens, the ice-covered volcano rising dramatically from deep green forests at the south end of the lake. The first recorded ascent from Spirit Lake was made in 1893 by Frederick Plummer and four others. Plummer was an avid mountaineer who produced the first detailed map of Mount Rainier, and in 1899 surveyed and mapped Mount Rainier Forest Reserve for the U. S. Geological Survey.

SILVER CREEK RANGER STATION

Outdoor clubs took a strong interest in Mount St. Helens, beginning with a climb by the Oregon Alpine Club in 1889. The Mazamas, from Portland, and the Mountaineers, from Seattle, led many trips to the mountain in subsequent years. One notable early event involved setting flares from the summits of St. Helens and three other volcanoes on July 4th, 1907.

George Williams, forest ranger at Spirit Lake, climbed Mount St. Helens twenty-one times, once in the record-breaking time of five hours and ten minutes round-trip from Spirit Lake. E. E. Robertson said of the feat: "On this occasion, in the company of his brother, the trip was purposefully made with the thought of making speed and considering the 6,500 foot climb from Spirit Lake to the summit, it is an achievement of stamina which probably has never been equaled."

Randle Ranger District

When Mount Rainier Forest Reserve was created in 1897, more than 50 settlers had already established homesteads in the Cowlitz River valley, within the reserve. The small town of Randle had emerged in the 1890s as a center of commerce for the pioneer families. The town was named for James L. Randle, its first postmaster, who had settled there in 1886. Randle's son Charles, hired initially as a ranger under the Department of the Interior, was the first forest service ranger stationed at Randle to oversee the Cowlitz Ranger District. In 1906, Randle transferred to the Wind River area and was replaced by Alfred B. Conrad, from the Nisqually Ranger District. With help from Nisqually ranger William McCullough, Conrad built the

JOHN KIRKPATRICK, RANGER FROM 1909 TO 1934

Silver Creek Ranger Station in 1907. The cabin became headquarters for the newly established Randle Ranger District in the same year. From 1908 until 1933, the district was part of Rainier National Forest.

In 1909 Alfred Conrad was replaced by John Kirkpatrick. Kirkpatrick chalked up many accomplishments during his twenty-three years as district ranger at Randle. Buildings were added to the administrative site, located a mile east of Randle and currently the headquarters of Cowlitz Valley Ranger District. Guard stations were established at Tower Rock by 1909, and the more remote Chain of Lakes in 1913. The first fire lookout on the district was constructed on Kiona Peak in 1917. In 1926 two other lookouts were built, one on Cispus Peak and one on Badger Peak. Early trail projects included the 1911 reconstruction of the Klickitat Trail, an old Indian travel route, and the building of a trail to Blue Lake in 1919.

Administrative duties also included the inspection of homestead claims, mining claims, grazing allotments, and timber sales. Most of the prospecting and mineral claim development was in the McCoy Creek area. Sheep allotments were established on ridges burned by the fire of 1902, including Juniper Ridge, Blue Lake Ridge, East Canyon Ridge, and Hamilton Buttes.

The earliest timber sales were for cedar in the Cispus River Valley. Cedar trees were felled, cut into shingle bolts, and floated downstream to mill locations. The first large commercial sale was made in 1909 to the Metcalf Shingle Company from Kelso. The company established a camp near Tower Rock Ranger Station, and continued to cut cedar in the area for several years. For a short time, Cispus Ranger District, with a staff of four men headquartered at Tower Rock, was administered separately.

In 1918, more than thirty-percent of the district burned in a tremendous wildfire known as the Cispus Burn. The small body of rangers and guards could do little to halt the fire. Army troops were sent from Fort Lewis to combat the blaze. Rains eventually put the fire out in the fall of the year.

In 1933, Randle Ranger District was added to Columbia National Forest. John Kirkpatrick retired the following year, and was replaced briefly by Harvey Welty, who had been the ranger at Trout Lake. Melvin M. Lewis took the job from 1935 to 1945. When Lewis retired, Harold Chriswell became district ranger.

The Forest Homestead Act

The creation of Mount Rainier Forest Reserve halted new settlement in the upper Cowlitz Valley until 1906, when the Forest Homestead Act (or "June 11th Act") again made land available. Homesteaders could claim up to 160 acres, provided the use was clearly agricultural. Claims were subject to approval by the forest supervisor.

In 1914, under considerable public pressure, Congress changed the forest boundaries to exclude the valley bottoms along the Cowlitz, where most earlier settlement had occurred. This action opened additional lands to homestead entry, causing the only real land rush the area had ever seen. By 1918, most claims had been patented. Many were sold almost immediately to timber companies.

Because of the potential for timber and land fraud, rangers and guards made rigorous examinations of all claims. This was an important duty of most rangers in the early days of the forest service, not only in the Cowlitz Valley area but in the other districts as well. Some claims were contested in court. Rangers and guards were occasionally called to testify in these cases.

CABIN ON STEEP HILLSIDE WITH FIR AND HEMLOCK TIMBER ON PROTESTED HOMESTEAD CLAIM, SEPTEMBER 26, 1907

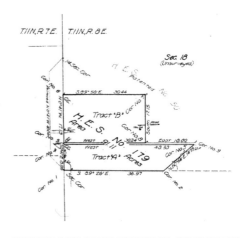

PLAT MAP, THOS. MUSIC HOMESTEAD, CISPUS VALLEY

"Reg. 1. Persons having valid claims under the public-land laws or legal titles to lands within forest reserves are free to occupy and enjoy their holdings, but must not interfere with the purposes for which the reserves are created, and must not cut timber or make use of forest-reserve land without a permit, except within the limits and for the actual development of their claims. Any other use will constitute trespass."

—*Gifford Pinchot*, THE USE BOOK, 1906

"The claim has the appearance of a permanent home in the making. The buildings are of simple construction though fairly comfortable and about all that could reasonably be expected under the circumstances... To my mind the good faith of the applicant has been fully shown... Hearing should not be ordered to determine the validity of the claim. There can be no doubt that the Claimant is complying and has complied all along with the requirements of the homestead law."

—*John Kirkpatrick, Forest Ranger*
April 11, 1918 letter to G. F. Allen, Forest Supervisor

THE CISPUS BURN NEAR FRENCH BUTTE IN 1922

Forests For the Future: Planting the Cispus Burn

"The two great forest fires of 1902 and 1918 in the Cispus-Mount Adams country had killed all tree growth on large areas and restocking of these had failed to take place naturally. The job of planting these with small tree seedlings was therefore started in 1920. The first of these areas to be planted was near the mouth of the North Fork of the Cispus River, about 15 miles southeast of Randle. During the next six years several thousand acres of these barren areas were planted by Forest Service crews. Mr. Isaac DeRosset of Randle supervised most of this work."

—*R. S. Jacobsen, District Ranger, 1953*

TREE PLANTING CREW

"Yeah, I planted trees. They're even cutting some of the trees I planted now. They're logging it already; on the Cispus. It was like a big burn, you know. When I started that and I was planting and having a good time, there was a leader going straight through, you know. And I was following the leader and kept the rest of the guys eight feet away from me. They had to keep everybody eight feet apart, you know. And you went right in a line and they followed right along: plant a tree and move on... a hoedag with a long shank on it. Cut down in, dig it on up, and put your tree in there. Oh yeah, we had to plant 400 of 'em. We had a little bag with a pack strapped on. Pull the tree out, they'd look at 'em and decide. They had roots on 'em about... a foot long... so I cut mine off to, oh, just about... seven or eight inches. They'd go down that hole there just fine. Pull the whole bit down and tamp it down..."

—*Hank Cheney, 1981 oral history interview*

"Used throughout the year by the district ranger as his headquarters. Improvements consist of a three-room log cabin, a post and split board barn 38x46, root house, woodshed and well. Twenty-seven acres are under fence. Six acres of this were used for hay land and twelve acres for pasture in 1913."

> —G. F. Allen, 1913 description of
> Skate Creek Ranger Station

Packwood Ranger District

When Mount Rainier Forest Reserve was created in 1897, the only community in the upper Cowlitz valley above Randle was then known as Sulphur Springs. In 1907, the Cowlitz Ranger District of Rainier National Forest was split into two smaller ranger districts. One of them became the Sulphur Springs Ranger District. Harry Cunningham was appointed as the first ranger of the district in 1908, initially making his headquarters in a cabin on

BILL SETHE WAS A FOREST SERVICE INSTITUTION CHARACTERIZED IN *TATOOSH* AND *SKYO*, TWO POPULAR BOOKS OF NONFICTION WRITTEN IN THE 1940S BY SEATTLE AUTHOR MARTHA HARDY. BILL RETIRED FROM THE RANGER POSITION IN 1947, HAVING SEEN THE FOREST SERVICE THROUGH A PERIOD OF GREAT CHANGE.

the homestead of Ed Dixon, north of present-day Packwood. Cunningham built the first ranger station at the Skate Creek administrative site in 1909.

The next year, the town of Lewis was established across the Cowlitz River, retaining that name until 1930, when it was changed to Packwood to avoid confusion with Fort Lewis. The ranger district was known both as Lewis Ranger District and Upper Cowlitz Ranger District in the years between 1910 and 1930. Until 1933, the ranger district was part of Rainier National Forest. In 1933 it was added to Columbia National Forest.

In 1910, Jules L. Hagon was hired as forest guard to assist Ranger Cunningham and was stationed all summer at the Davis Coal Mines on Summit Creek. William Sethe was hired as a forest guard in 1911, eventually succeeding Cunningham as ranger four years later. Bill's brother Fritz worked as assistant ranger at Wind River in the early days, and brother Herb was a ranger at Mount Rainier National Park.

BERRY PATCH GUARD STATION

The original ranger station burned to the ground in a 1919 fire, and a new house was built. In 1923, the station was moved into an old store in the town of Lewis. This served as Lewis Ranger Station until 1930, when an office and warehouse were built on newly acquired property at the east end of town, on the main highway. A residence was added to the complex in 1931. Until 1998, when the ranger district consolidated with Randle, this was the site of Packwood Ranger Station.

During the early years of Packwood Ranger District, the principal activity was trail construction. The Skate Creek, Cowlitz Pass, and Johnson Creek Trails were among the earliest projects completed. A log cabin at Packwood Lake, built in 1910 for a power development company camp, became one of the first guard stations in the district. Berry Patch Guard Station, at Chambers Lake, was built in 1916. Remote Hawkeye Fire Lookout was the first to be built on the ranger district, in 1927. Clear Fork Guard Station, in today's La Wis Wis Campground, was built in 1928.

In the early 1920s, Packwood Ranger District supported eleven sheep allotments and three cattle ranges. By 1937, the district maintained 411 miles of trail, 116

"These peaks of the Goat Rocks are not high as Western peaks go; they are around 8200 feet. But no mountain I have been on, not even Adams, creates the same feeling of height. The highest point on Gilbert Peak is like a crow's nest at the top of a long mast. There is not room for more than a dozen people. Up there one has the feeling that the nest rides at the top of the heavens and rules over the whole domain of the Cascades."

—William O. Douglas, OF MEN AND MOUNTAINS, 1949

PACKWOOD LAKE, A POPULAR FISHING DESTINATION

miles of telephone line, ten fire lookouts, five guard stations, employed twelve forest guards, and maintained a fine string of pack mules.

PLANTING TROUT FINGERLINGS, 1930s

"During the summer of 1913 while fording the river on a strange horse, the Forest Supervisor got into trouble and his horse fell backwards ducking the Supervisor in the water. It was rumored that this affair caused him to agree that a bridge was needed... The Forest Service first planned on constructing a horse bridge only. Settlers offered six hundred dollars in donations if the Forest Service would build a bridge wide enough for a wagon... The Forest Supervisor reconsidered. A suspension bridge with a 180-foot span and a 120-foot approach of logs and split puncheon was built."

—Claire Wood, Packwood, memo dated March 4, 1935

COWLITZ RIVER SUSPENSION BRIDGE - A COOPERATIVE VENTURE WITH THE LOCAL COMMUNITY. THE BRIDGE WAS DESTROYED BY FLOODING IN 1933.

Packwood Ranger District included the crest of the Cascade Range from Mount Rainier National Park south to Walupt Lake. Early recreation use of the backcountry included hunting and fishing trips by local families as well as more formal outings organized by outdoor clubs from Seattle, Yakima, and other communities. The Seattle-based Mountaineers, for example, organized a three-week outing in 1911 that traversed the mountains from Mount Rainier south to Mount Adams and the Columbia River. In 1931, Goat Rocks Primitive Area was established for its scenic and recreational values. An increase in backcountry recreation led to reductions in grazing, where uses were in conflict.

Mountain lakes and streams teeming with fish attracted sport fishermen from outside the local area. Packwood Lake, renowned for its native rainbow trout and spectacular scenery, was a popular destination for anglers. A resort was established at the lake in 1921, growing over the years from a tent camp to a cluster of cabins around a lodge, where boats could be rented and meals obtained. In the late 1920s and 1930s, trout were planted throughout the backcountry of the ranger district to enhance recreational fishing. A salmon hatchery was built on the Clear Fork Cowlitz River in 1926 by the State Food Fish Department to raise fish for planting in other areas of western Washington.

Mineral Ranger District

Mineral Ranger District initially incorporated the Puyallup and Nisqually River drainages and was originally known as Nisqually Ranger District. William A. McCullough was the first district ranger, appointed under the General Land

COMPANY MINING TOWN OF LADD. COVERED RAILROAD TRACK AND COAL BUNKERS IN BACKGROUND

Office in 1904 and serving until his retirement in 1922. McCullough administered the district from his home near Ashford. In 1906 the Ashford Addition, lying west of Mineral, was added to Nisqually Ranger District.

The Ashford Addition, also known as Tilton Ranger District and the "Mineral Addition," was administered separately from 1913 to 1922. For several years an office in Morton was used. When it was again combined with Nisqually Ranger District, Tilton District Ranger Jules Hagon replaced William McCullough as ranger of the new Mineral Ranger District. Hagon continued to work from an office established in Mineral.

The district was part of Rainier National Forest until 1933, when it was added to Snoqualmie National Forest. The first official ranger station was developed by the Civilian Conservation Corps near Mineral in 1934. In 1969 the ranger district was dissolved and administration transferred to Gifford Pinchot National Forest.

JULES HAGON

The name of the district comes from the community of Mineral, indicating one of the resources of commercial importance in the early days. Four miles west of Mineral was the town of Ladd, adjacent to the forest boundary along East Creek. Ladd was a company town, established by 1905 as the headquarters of an anthracite coal mining operation. The Phoenix Mine was the largest development, with a network of tunnels extending over a mile into forest service lands. A massive landslide in 1919 closed the mine, which had employed 250 men during peak operations.

By December 1910, the first commercial timber sale of note was underway along the Nisqually River. This was a shingle bolt sale, where cutters took cedar trees that grew close to the river, bucking them into sections called bolts. When winter rains created high water, the bolts were floated downstream to a shingle mill.

FIREFIGHTER WITH A BACKPACK WATER CAN AND PUMP SPRAYER

Fires and Firefighting

"A severe fire that occurred in the early days of the Forest Service was the devastating Cispus Fire which started September 2, 1902 about 25 miles south of Randle and burned over approximately 800,000 acres destroying several billion board feet of virgin timber. This fire is thought to have been started by a mining prospector who wished to get rid of the brush and fallen trees in the area he planned to work to make travel easier. Some idea of the attitude toward the conservation of the Forests at that time can be gotten from the fact that one homesteader hoped that this raging fire would reach his land and burn the timber that stood on it in order to make clearing easier."

—Reuben Jacobsen, HISTORY OF THE FOREST SERVICE AND
THE NATIONAL FOREST IN EASTERN LEWIS COUNTY, 1953

"It is 2 P.M. when I strike the McCoy Creek trail, I eat my lunch here and watch the progress of the fire for more than two hours. It is a fearful sight as it leaps from tree to tree and spreads out in a solid wall of fire 20' to 40' high along the side of the Mtn. Causes one to realize more and more the insignificance of the very best human efforts that can be put forth when pitted against the irresistible forces of the natural elements. Man and the best that is in him is of small consequence..."

—Ranger John Kirkpatrick,
June 25 entry in diary account of the Cispus Fire of 1918

Instructions for Smoke Chasers

You have been selected and trained for smoke chasing. You will work generally in two man units. As a smoke chaser you are subject to call any time of the day or night. Your job is to find and put out small fires, and to do this you must be thoroughly familiar with the use of a map and compass, also the country surrounding your camp. You should be equipped with caulked or hob-nail shoes and they should be kept in good condition at all times.

Before starting for the fire be sure that you receive all the necessary information as to its location. Also that the location is definitely marked on your map. You will be equipped with a complete two man outfit which includes all the tools necessary for suppressing a small fire. Emergency rations and mess equipment will be furnished to sustain yourself for two days.

—*Ross Shepeard, 1935*

SMOKECHASER HEADS UP THE TRAIL WITH GEAR STRAPPED TO A WOODEN "CLACK BOARD" PACKFRAME

Jim had been on the Cispus Fire. He said one day the fire made a big run, and the next morning Mr. Allen said to him "Jim, I want you to take the best damn man you can find and go see where in hell that fire went to."

—*Harry White*

A Ranger Gives His Life

"The only fire of importance of recent years was the so-called Yacolt Fire of 1902... Between 30 and 40 lives were lost in this fire which covered approximately 7 townships of densely timbered country, of which 2 1/2 townships are now within the Forest."

—*Arthur R. Wilcox, 1911 report*

"The fall of 1902 was the great fire of the Wind and Lewis rivers. It swept through the timber driven by a strong east wind, and nothing could have stopped it after it got started. The smoke from it even darkened the skies where I was on the Nisqually."

—*John Schmitz, 1949 letter to K.P. Cecil*

The Dole fire of 1929 burned 60,000 acres on the forest, reburning a portion of the Yacolt fire of 1902. A group of Forest Service firefighters was burned over while attempting to fight this fire, taking refuge in a mine shaft on Copper Creek, in the East Fork Lewis River drainage. One of these men, Hemlock District Ranger James H. Huffman, died as a result of his ordeal.

Spirit Lake District Ranger Al Wang described how, on September 15, 1929, the crew was searching for spot fires near Silver Star Mountain when the humidity dropped and east winds began blowing at 50-60 mph. Because the smoke was coming down in dense clouds, they had no idea of where the main fire was nor how fast it was traveling. They recognized the danger and found shelter in a mine shaft along Copper Creek.

The crew spent several hours packing food supplies and equipment the quarter-mile from their camp to the mine shaft. Wang wrote:

"It was fairly obvious now that we would be burned out sometime during the day and our efforts were directed to moving these supplies to the tunnel... Smoke and heat were increasingly irritating and it seemed impossible to get sufficient air to breathe."

At 5:30 that evening Huffman, Al Wang, and Bob Lambert made the last trip from the mine shaft back to camp for their bedrolls, estimating that the fire was about a mile away. Continues Wang:

"By the time we got to the camp we noted that spot fires were starting in our vicinity and were spreading very rapidly. We got our beds and started the return trip. This was a race with the fire, which was starting spontaneously all around us and seemingly closing in from every direction. The last 100 yards or so was a race for life and we made the tunnel a half minute before the full force of the fire swept over it."

The men hung blankets at the mouth of the mine shaft, and took turns throwing water over the blankets to keep them from burning. They spent five and one-half hours in the cold wet mine shaft, while the worst of the fire burned over them. They emerged at 11:30 that night, but could not travel because of the danger from falling snags. The next day, Wang noted:

"The smoke was almost impenetrable and the day would have been totally dark, except that it was lighted sufficiently by blazing snags to enable us to get around without lights."

The crew had to pack out under very smoky conditions, with blowing ash making breathing even more difficult, and Huffman was so weakened at this point that it took him nine hours to hike the seven miles to Yacolt, the nearest road. He died within a month, probably from pneumonia brought on by their ordeal.

Communication

"I am sure that we all appreciate now the desirability of having a complete telephone system throughout the Forest. The history of the discovery of one fire on the Columbia during the past season is interesting as it affects the telephone question. A fire occurred at the north end of Spirit Lake... at noon of August 16. This fire was seen early in the afternoon of August 16 by three Guards, all of whom reported the fire in the following manner:

Guard Skaar, located approximately 25 miles from the fire, rode 23 miles in to Guler in order that he might report the fire to the Portland office.

Guard Wetherall, located approximately 30 miles from the fire, rode fifteen miles to the Hemlock Ranger Station to report the fire to the District Ranger.

HANGING PHONE LINE ON SNAG

Guard Lewis, located approximately 26 miles due south of the fire, rode seven miles to the Government Soda Springs in order that he might report the fire by telephone to the District Ranger."

—H. O. Stabler, 1911 Fire Report

"The Mt. Adams R.D. had a very extensive telephone line system, both duplex and grounded... K.C. was very insistent that line work was always the first order of business and of the highest quality. Virtually every trail shelter and camp was served by some sort of line. Smokechasers could patch into a line about anywhere and communicate with lookouts for a location fix. A fix was usually made by mirror flashing from a climbable tree or forest opening... I believe there was something like 400 miles or more of line. One year I hung most of this after a very severe winter and have the leg scars to this day."

—Bob Larse, 1989 interview

"Plans for the experimental use of radio communication on the Columbia this season are now being consummated and the actual work of installation of the central station is well under way... Between 5 and 7 portable radio sets, equipped to receive voice and send code will be allocated to different parts of the Forest. These sets will weigh about 75 pounds each and are designed so as to divide the weight into 3 units which will permit transporting either by pack-horse or back-packing man. The object of placing the radio equipment on the Columbia this year is to determine the feasibility of using radio communication under actual Forest conditions."

—*J. R. Bruckart*, SIX TWENTY-SIX, *1930*

"I am not skeptical any more. The sets are working, schedule after schedule, the inexperienced men are getting their messages through... It is yet too early in the game to make a comparison between radio communication and emergency telephone lines but I do know now that we will establish communication with isolated trail crews and fire camps much quicker by radio, and we know that quick action is what counts on fires in the old burns such as we have on the Columbia."

—*J. M. Mann,*
SIX TWENTY-SIX, *1931*

Fire Lookouts

Red Mountain, one of the few places where a fire lookout still stands, was also the first point on the forest to have a lookout. The earliest lookout on Red Mountain was built in 1910 by Fritz Sethe, assistant ranger at Hemlock, and this was replaced in 1935 by a standard L-4 cabin. The lookout tower that stands at the site today was built in 1959, replacing the 1930s lookout.

RED MOUNTAIN'S FIRST LOOKOUT, BUILT IN 1910

The Highest Lookout

MOUNT ADAMS LOOKOUT, 1922

Mount Adams, with an elevation of 12,276 feet, has the country's highest fire lookout on its summit. Construction began on the lookout in 1918, when the lumber was moved by packhorses to a point below Crescent Glacier. In 1919 four men, including Art Jones, hauled the material the remainder of the way to the summit using a system of counterbalanced sleds. Construction began in 1920, and Art Jones and Adolph Schmid completed the building in 1921. They manned the lookouts in 1922, then Jones and Chaffin Johnson took the job in 1923.

When Jones and Johnson reached the fire lookout on July 1, 1923, only one corner of the roof was visible, and they had to do a little digging to find the front door. The 1,800 pounds of food and fuel they would need for the summer had to be packed to the summit on their backs.

One of the things the men discovered about living above 12,000 feet is that storms can be a little severe. One particularly memorable storm occurred in August of 1923, when Jones and Johnson described balls of fire leaping from the end of their hastily severed telephone wire. The hail came down so violently it broke a window in the lookout. But the finale came when the door of the lookout was blasted off by

COLDWATER PEAK LOOKOUT UNDER CONSTRUCTION IN 1936 WITH MOUNT ST. HELENS

SLEEPING BEAUTY LOOKOUT

a bolt of lightning, reducing the hinges to a mass of melted metal. After the storm passed they found entire sections of telephone wire had melted. That was the last summer that Jones and Johnson spent on the summit of Mount Adams, and by 1924 the decision was made to abandon the lookout that had taken four years to construct.

Strawberry Lookout

"Bill Roe, who hangs his hat on the peak of Strawberry and calls it 'home,' will soon have the new L. O. station ready to move into. Bill has had a tough job making his own lumber out of twisty mountain Hemlock in his one man sawmill. When Bill gets a board made, he spikes it in place, so it won't curl up and crawl away while he is making another. Shingles were made at Spirit Lake and packed out 12 miles. Bill is making everything else except the glass for the windows and the knob for the door. (Can't somebody get a glass blower for Bill? - Ed.)"

THE COLUMBIA RECORD, *1926*

BILL ROE AT STRAWBERRY MOUNTAIN LOOKOUT, 1930

THE MOUNTAINEERS' 1911 ASCENT OF MOUNT ADAMS

CLIMBERS ON MOUNT ADAMS

Mountain Vacations: Early Recreation

The first documented ascent of Mount St. Helens was in 1853, by a group consisting of Thomas Dryer, the founder of the Portland *Oregonian* newspaper, and three companions named Wilson, Drew, and Smith. A full account of their ascent was published in the *Oregonian* in September 1853. Starting out at Vancouver and continuing to the Lewis River they followed the route opened by George McClellan only a month earlier. From their camp above the Lewis River it took the group two days to reach the summit from the south side... and five days to return, on horseback, to Vancouver.

HAROLD SAMUELSON ON MOUNT
ST. HELENS, 1920s

The first ascent of Mount Adams in 1854 was via the North Cleaver route by members of a party constructing a military road over Naches Pass, between Fort Walla Walla and Puget Sound. In fact, the construction of this road had been one of the tasks assigned to George McClellan in 1853, but he passed it on to civilians. The group consisted of A. G. Aiken, E. J. Allen, Andrew Birge, and B. F. Shaw. They approached the mountain from the northeast, a point from which the North Cleaver route would have appeared the logical choice. The South Climb route, the most popular climbing route today, was first climbed in 1866.

The Mountaineers, the Mazamas, and the Cascadians all staged "outings," or group ascents on Mount Adams and Mount St. Helens in the teens and twenties. One such outing sponsored

by the Mountaineers in 1917 began at Castle Rock, included the ascent of both Mount St. Helens and Mount Adams, and ended on the Columbia River at Cooks—a "hike" of 125 miles.

Government Mineral Springs

In 1910 S. D. Fox and the Star Brewing Company of Portland began construction of a 50-room hotel at the soda springs near Trapper Creek, later known as Government Mineral Springs. This popular resort boasted bath houses, Iron Mike Bubbling Springs, a dance pavilion, a store and ice cream parlor, hiking trails, goldfish ponds, flower gardens, and a camping area. Early advertisements for the resort claimed the mineral water spas were capable of curing physical ailments such as gallstones, rheumatism, diabetes and anemia, as well as stomach, liver, kidney, skin, and nervous disorders. A new wing was built on the hotel in the 1920s, but in 1935 Government Mineral Springs Hotel burned to the ground.

RECREATION HAS TAKEN MANY FACES ON THE FOREST, FROM MOUNTAIN CLIMBING TO DANCE PAVILIONS, AND FROM PRIMITIVE HIKING TRAILS TO SUMMER HOMES. A SUMMER HOME TRACT WAS DEVELOPED AT GOVERNMENT MINERAL SPRINGS IN THE 1920s.

"In the long, clear days of summer the Forest is a playground for both the farmer and the city dweller... Mountain climbers scale the snowy peaks, tourists of less strenuous habits camp along the highways, fishermen follow the streams, and the bugles of Boy Scouts echo in the mountain glen."

—1920 Rainier National Forest brochure

A FAMILY RELAXES AT THEIR CAMP AFTER A DAY OF HUCKLEBERRY PICKING, 1930

INDIAN GUARD LOUIS CHARLES AND YAKAMA BERRY PICKERS AT SURPRISE LAKES

Traditional Uses: The Handshake Treaty

"The Twin Buttes territory has been the traditional Indian berry picking ground for many years... Families use the same spots, the same teepee poles season after season... The prime objective of the Indians' trek to the mountains is to gather berries and they are now and have been for years established in the place of their choice, the one place on the Columbia Forest where their needs can be easily satisfied."

—J. R. Bruckart, January, 1932 letter

"The Indians for generations have gone to this forest in the fall of the year to gather wild huckleberries. These berries they can and dry for winter food... up to a year or so ago the huckleberry patch was left largely to Indians. However, during the past two or three years of economic depression the jobless white people have flocked to this forest in increasing numbers for the sake of the little money that might be earned from the sale of the berries. When the Indians went to the berry patch this year they found their old familiar territory preempted by thousands of white people. They protested to the Forest Officials. The Indians set up the claim that this area had belonged to their forefathers and by a certain clause in the treaty of 1855 the right to gather berries, hunt and fish had been reserved to the Indians."

—C. R. Whitlock, Superintendent, Yakima Indian Agency, 1932 letter

A series of councils were held between 1928 and 1936, where the Forest Supervisor of the Columbia National Forest and the District Ranger of the Mount Adams Ranger District met with representatives of various bands of the Yakama Indian

TRADITIONAL METHOD OF DRYING HUCKLEBERRIES WITH THE HEAT OF A LOG FIRE

Nation to discuss the situation. Over the years three different Forest Supervisors (F. V. Horton, J. R. Bruckart, and K. P. Cecil) and two District Rangers (H. A. Welty and K. C. Langfield) participated in these meetings, and all of them were sympathetic to the concerns expressed by the Indians.

"At the request of some of the Indians I met with them last summer, and at this meeting they spoke at length of their treaty rights and how these rights were in effect being nullified by the

TRIBAL REPRESENTATIVES AND FOREST SERVICE OFFICIALS MEET AT COLD SPRINGS INDIAN CAMP, 1936

CHIEF WILLIAM YALLUP AND FOREST SUPERVISOR K. P. CECIL AT COUNCIL MEETING IN THE SAWTOOTH BERRY FIELDS, 1936

CARTOON FROM *COLUMBIAN*, AUG. 15, 1936

local game authorities and the influx of the white people into the country around Twin Buttes where they had for generations been accustomed to come and gather berries... Many of the officials of Skamania County are in sympathy with the Indians, as I am myself, in their attempt to retain what they believe to be their ancient rights secured to them by this treaty."

—J. R. Bruckart, 1932 letter to Regional Forester

Forest Supervisor J. R. Bruckart agreed in 1932 to set aside a portion of the Sawtooth Huckleberry Fields for the exclusive use of Indian people, and also to reserve the four campgrounds in the huckleberry fields for exclusive Indian use. This agreement was formalized by a handshake between Bruckart and Chief William Yallup, chief of the Kamiltpah band.

A 1936 USFS brochure for the Twin Buttes Recreation Area contains a map which shows a portion of the huckleberry fields as "reserved for Indians." The brochure also contains the following narrative:

"Hundreds of Indians make annual pilgrimages to these huckleberry fields. Their use of the area is assured by an old treaty which gives them the right to gather roots and berries in this region for all time. A portion of the berry fields have been reserved for their use. The public is asked to respect their rights."

CCC SPIKE CAMP IN YACOLT BURN

The Civilian Conservation Corps

"I propose to create a Civilian Conservation Corps to be used in simple work, not interfering with normal employment, and confining itself to forestry, the prevention of soil erosion, flood control and similar projects. I call your attention to the fact that this type of work is of definite, practical value, not only through the prevention of great present financial loss, but also as a means of creating future national wealth."

—*Franklin D. Roosevelt, March 21, 1933*
message to First Session, 73rd Congress

The Great Depression was a time of great hardship for many Americans. Roosevelt believed that providing honest work for unemployed men would restore their sense of pride in themselves, while conserving and replenishing our natural resources.

There were nine regional CCC areas, each commanded by a U.S. Army general. After joining, the enrollees were assigned to a company, sent to an army post for two to four weeks of physical conditioning, and then sent on to the camps. The camps were under the command of regular U.S. Army officers, but during working hours the enrollees were supervised by the responsible work agency, such as the U. S. Forest Service.

The CCC was made up of different categories of enrollees. The largest group were the young men, or Juniors as they were called. They were unmarried, between the ages of 18 and 25, and were selected from families on relief. Enrollment was for a period of six months, and if their work was acceptable they could re-enlist for another six months. They were paid $30 per month, $25 of which was sent home to help their families.

SIOUXON CAMP 1933, IN WIND RIVER VALLEY

CREW FOREMAN AT CAMP HEMLOCK

Another group of enrollees were the Local Experienced Men, or LEMs. These men were hired from the local communities and were chosen because of their experience. Each camp was usually assigned eight LEMs, who served as project leaders. LEMs had no age restrictions, they could be married, and were permitted to live at home if the camp was nearby.

Of Definite, Practical Value

"Our day began with reveille at 5:30, breakfast at 6:00, roll call and sick call at 6:30, and work call at 7:00. Those not confined to camp because of real or faked illness boarded the trucks and were transported to the various work projects in the area. Several maintenance and improvement programs went on simultaneously: road and trail

EXPLAINING REFORESTATION PRINCIPLES TO A GROUP OF CCC ENROLLEES

THE CCC BOYS AT PETERSON PRAIRIE WITH THEIR CAMP MASCOT

CAMP LOWER CISPUS, NEAR RANDLE

construction, stringing telephone wires, erecting bridges and fire lookouts, and felling snags, burning slash, and planting trees on the Yacolt burn."

—*Edwin G. Hill, describing Sunset CCC camp* IN THE SHADOW OF THE MOUNTAIN, *1990*

"With the advent of the New Deal, the work program of the Forest Service and other public agencies were vastly expanded. First by the Civilian Conservation Corps. The first six months of 1933 the Columbia was allocated nine 200-man camps. Projects were reforestation, constructing fire breaks along with snag

TRAIL CONSTRUCTION BY CCC CREW

UNLOADING FIRE TOOLS

felling, road and campground construction and other needed improvements.

With the abundant manpower available, construction of truck trails, snag felling fire breaks, horse trails, campgrounds and many other improvement projects were pushed aggressively."

—J. R. Bruckart, ca. 1972,
MEMOIRS OF JOHN "RAY"
BRUCKART, SR.

"War has been declared on the wolf at the door and all through the land, from the ranks of the younger unemployed, men are being recruited to work in the woods this summer for $30 a month plus food, clothing and bedding."

—L. G. Richards, OREGONIAN,
May 3, 1933

Trial and Error Method

"It must be remembered that many of the enrolled men know nothing whatever about the handling of simple tools which they are expected to use. Much of the necessary knowledge must necessarily be gained through 'absorption' and by the 'trial and error' method. However, some simple lessons in the use of these tools will make the work easier for the men, will cause more work to be done, and will result in fewer tools being ruined."

—C. J. Buck, Regional Forester,
CIRCULAR NO. 101,
June 22, 1933

"Thanks to the foreman and local boys, the Chicago men were given instructions in how to use such tools as saws and axes and in a very short time these fellows will be able to use them efficiently. Every man now has a good coat of tan and some real hard muscles and is full of pep. With this combination

FELLING SNAGS WITH A MISERY WHIP, TO REDUCE FIRE HAZARD

THE CCC CONSTRUCTED MANY MILES OF ROAD THROUGHOUT THE NATIONAL FOREST

there is only one result, a successful work program. To date, the amount of work that has been done is as follows: 50 miles of trail betterment, 38 miles of telephone lines, 17 miles of truck trails betterment, and 1 mile of truck trail constructed."

—Clarence Peterson, Peterson Prairie CCC Camp superintendent, 1933

"Tight-packed bales of 200,000 or so seedlings are rushed here from the Hemlock nursery on the Wind River. The roots of the young plants are carefully packed in wet moss or shingle row, and the whole protected with burlap for packing on the train of ornery government mules that winds its way by trail five miles further up the river to a typical planter's camp.

Here the bundles are divided among the 40 men making up three planting crews. Each man is armed with a grubbing hoe and a bag containing some 30 pounds of young fir plants. Lining up at intervals of eight feet, the crew of 10 to 15 starts up the hill. Every eight feet each man stops and sinks his hodag into the soil with his right hand, carefully sets the young seedling upright in the hole, roots pointing straight down, and tamps the earth firmly around the babe."

—L. G. Richards, OREGONIAN, May 3, 1933

A PACK STRING HAULING SEEDLINGS TO PLANTING CREWS

"MINNIE" PACKING MATTRESSES TO THE CCC SPIKE
CAMP AT TEXAS GULCH

Camp Hemlock (Camp F-40)

"Work completed: Construction of ranger station residences, L. O. houses, garages, storage warehouses, training school Bldg's, water systems, bridges, road, truck trails, telephone line, fire break, maintenance of truck trails, roads, and telephone line. Fire suppression and pre suppression."

—*A. W. Stockman,* ccc
inspection report,
Sept. 15, 1941

"I want to go on record as stating that in my opinion no phase of the CCC program is more important than our relationship with youth. I am hopeful that as time passes we can do even more than we are doing today to assist youth to become self-supporting. I am not a believer in coddling youngsters and so long as I am director I intend to do everything I can to help young men develop self-reliance and pride in their ability to make their own way in the world."

—*Robert Fechner, Director, CCC,* american forests, *April 1939*

The CCC was disbanded in 1942. During its nine-year run the accomplishments of the CCC were nothing less than spectacular. The enduring legacy of the CCC, most easily seen in our national forests and parks, has benefited every American.

CCC PLANTING CREW HEADS UP THE TRAIL INTO YACOLT BURN

CCC ROAD CONSTRUCTION

CCC ROAD CONSTRUCTION

TRAINING WOMEN LOOKOUTS IN THE USE OF A FIRE FINDER DURING WWII

The Forest During World War II

Aircraft Warning Service

"As you no doubt know, we are in the process of organizing an Aircraft Warning Service in Oregon and Washington. The posts outside of the U. S. Forests are being organized through the State Defense Commissions. As the Forests cover a great deal of this area it is necessary that we establish a number of Observation Posts within their boundaries. Due to the many problems involved, it is intended to hold the number to a minimum."

—Major R. E. Carlgren, Army Air Corps, July 30, 1941, letter

Japanese Medium Bomber
Mitsubishi Type I MB
"Betty"

PLAYING CARDS WERE USED BY SPOTTERS TO MEMORIZE AIRCRAFT SILHOUETTES

"I would not trade my experience in isolation for any other, though it lasted for nine months instead of one or two. It started in October, 1942 when it was decided to use Red Mountain, a peak 4,974 feet high in the Wind River District of the Columbia National Forest as an Aircraft Warning Service post, a high altitude weather station, and a lookout combined. When Larry and I were asked if we would care to take it over, we agreed that it was exactly the job for us.

After the first two or three weeks, we had settled down to a routine, and were learning to sleep at odd hours. We were on twenty-four hour duty, and with some experimenting we found that six hour shifts from two to eight and so on around the clock worked out best for us. Our days had

ALWILDA "BILLIE" WEBB, WORKING AT FLATTOP LOOKOUT

ALWILDA "BILLIE" WEBB, FLATTOP LOOKOUT, HIGH ABOVE THE TROUT LAKE VALLEY. WEBB MARRIED FOREST SUPERVISOR K. P. CECIL AT THE LOOKOUT IN 1949

no beginnings or ends, but were a series of telephone and radio check calls, weather readings, and watches, around and around the clock."

—Mary Rakestraw, AWS Observer, Red Mountain Lookout, 1942-1943

"By the ninth of December we had thirteen feet of snow, as nearly as we could estimate it, and orders for the winter conduct of the station began to come in over the telephone... It was not so much that we resented being told to do impossible things like keeping paths shoveled between buildings, clearing the roofs of ice, cutting steps in the steep slopes and covering them with ashes, and the telephone line free of its garland of frost—and these things were impossible—it was the cheerful voice from the Ranger Station commenting, 'After all, it will give you something to do,' that added insult to injury."

—Mary Rakestraw, AWS Observer, Red Mountain Lookout, 1942-194

"It was in August, I think, that I almost missed a B-17 flying low enough directly overhead for the wing markings to be visible. I was on watch inside and couldn't hear it above the sound of a twenty-five mile east wind."

—Mary Rakestraw, AWS Observer, Red Mountain Lookout 1942-1943

SIOUXON PEAK LOOKOUT, 1939

Fire Lookouts

"When I learned in the autumn of 1942 that the United States Forest Service planned to employ women the following year, I knew that I had found my wartime service for summer vacations: I should be a lookout, or forest guard, on some mountain peak... We learned how to meet the public as representatives of the Forest Service; how to operate a portable two-way radio; how to replace batteries and a burned-out fuse in a telephone; how to use and care for tools; how to read a compass; how to detect and located smokes; how to read section maps; and how to use the firefinder, the lookout's chief too... The lookout is expected to wash his windows after every rain or fog and at regular intervals during dry weather. This was no small task at Flattop, where I had fourteen windows in my living quarters and two glass-enclosed rooms, probably 6 by 6 feet and 10 by 10 feet, for the firefinders. But one cannot see smoke through streaked or rain-spotted windows... And of course housekeeping takes some time, even for one person, when it includes splitting kindling, cooking on a wood stove, baking bread, and doing the laundry with tub and washboard... One learns to be economical with water carried up from a spring. With the same water I have, in turn, shampooed my hair, washed my clothes, scrubbed the woodwork and mopped the floor. Then I have watered the nearest lilies or settled the dust near the cabin... As a war secrecy measure, both the evening forecast and my five o'clock report were made in code."

—*Ella Clark,* NATIONAL GEOGRAPHIC MAGAZINE, *July 1946*

"The packer with two mules arrived and dropped off my supplies after which he left leaving me as the only human for some twenty or more miles around. My link to civilization was a groundline telephone.

My time on Spencer Butte was one of the more enjoyable periods of my life... There were several lightning storms, during one the lookout received a strike. A blinding flash followed by a millisecond of slight crackling sound then a tremendous thunderclap. Burnt Peak called to tell me that my lookout had been struck. He didn't need to."

—Earl Johnson

"I have played a part in the old custodial days. The days of No. 9 telephone wire strung mile after mile and maintained for our communication everywhere. The days of backpacking and horse work. We had clack boards for our fire packs and even used the heavy old hoedags for fire line construction. The Stonebridge lantern was in our fire caches. They were the ingenious folding candle lantern from World War I. We had 10-man fire cache boxes. Most important were the great system of lookouts and fire guards. That was before radio communication, radar, plastic, ball point pens, credit cards, computers, and television."

—H. C. Chriswell, Randle District Ranger, 1945-1950, MEMOIRS, 1989

"I Want You to build a Lookout House": with these words District Ranger Al Wang, Spirit Lake District, sent me to Smith Creek Butte in the fall of 1930 with instructions to build a lookout house atop a 12 foot tower, already built. The house was a prefabricated one built by the Aladdin Company of Portland. It came in packages designed for back packing on a horse. It had all packages numbered and cross referenced in the plans. As the packer brought in the packaged lumber, the house began to take shape. I had no previous carpenter experience."

—Carlos T. (Tom) Brown, 1979

Roll Call of Stations

In the 1940s there was a so-called "Roll Call of Stations" during the fire season. All lookout points on the forest were connected by telephone through switchboards at ranger stations and major guard stations, where dispatchers could call up all the lookout stations in their group. The following is a "roll call" of all lookouts constructed on the forest:

MARTHA HARDY'S POPULAR 1946 BOOK *TATOOSH* DESCRIBED HER EXPERIENCES AS A WARTIME LOOKOUT

WIND RIVER DISTRICT

Mowich, Observation Peak, Siouxon Peak, Termination, Silver Star Mountain, Dog Mountain, Sisters Rock, Point 3670, Big Huckleberry Mountain, Bunker Hill, Gumboot Mountain, Lookout Mountain, Grassy Knoll, Green, Red Mountain, Saturday Rock, Summit, West Point, Horseshoe Ridge

MOUNT ADAMS DISTRICT

Little Baldy Peak, Little Huckleberry, Monte Cristo, East Flattop Mountain, West Flattop Mountain, Sleeping Beauty, Burnt Peak, Hungry Peak, Twin Buttes, Steamboat Mountain, Mount Adams, Summit Prairie, Council Bluff, Switchback, Breezy Point ELO, Madcat ELO

SPIRIT LAKE DISTRICT

Mount Mitchell, Mount Margaret, Strawberry, Coldwater, Huffman Peak, Clear Creek, Smith Creek Butte, Mount St. Helens, Lam Mountain, Spencer Butte, West Point, House Rock ELO

RANDLE DISTRICT

Burley Mountain, Langille Peak, Sunrise Peak, French Butte, Ferrous Point, Badger Peak, Tongue Mountain ELO, McCoy Peak ELO, Cispus Point, Pompey Peak, Trail's End, Watch Mountain, Kiona Peak, Hamilton Buttes, Midway, Vanson Peak

PACKWOOD DISTRICT

South Point, Nannie Peak, Goat Ridge, Lost Lake, Tatoosh Ridge, Dry Creek, Smith Butte, Hawkeye, Lakeview Mountain, Tumac

MINERAL DISTRICT

High Rock, Glacierview, Mount Beljica, Gobbler's Knob, The Rockies, Stahl Mountain, Pleasant Valley, Newaukum, Huckleberry, West Fork.

THE IRON CREEK TIMBER SALE, AN EXPERIMENT IN BLOCK CUTTING

Post-War Forest Service

Timber Sales

"The Army needed an enormous amount of lumber. It was necessary for the lumber used for certain purposes to have the proper tensile strength. Testing proved the slow-growing timber of this region was the best that could be obtained. Prior to this time there had been very few Forest Service timber sales, these were small special use sales of posts, poles, etc. When the lumber was needed for the Army the Forest Service policy was changed and they began making timber sales. At first only a small amount of timber was sold for local mills but as the demand became greater more timber was sold. These large amounts had to come from higher in the mountains where no roads existed so the only feasible way to get the timber cut was to make sales large enough to justify the purchaser making roads, the road expense being deducted from the sale price."

—*Packwood on the March*, PACKWOOD COMMUNITY STUDY, 1953-1954

"World War II, which caused a severe drain of timber on the private land out of state to the extent that it has been entirely depleted on a large percent of this forest area, has brought the logging industry into the National Forests. Up to this time the income to the Federal Government from the sale of timber on the Randle and Packwood Districts amounted to not more than a thousand dollars annually."

—*R. S. Jacobsen, Randle District Ranger, 1953*

J. NEILS LUMBER COMPANY CREW USING EARLY TWO-MAN CHAINSAW, MOUNT ADAMS DISTRICT, 1940s

There were four war time timber sales on the Mount Adams Ranger District. The J. Neils Lumber Company had a railroad logging operation on the east side between 1942 and 1946. Broughton Lumber Company was awarded a timber sale in the Little White Salmon drainage. H. D. Hollenbeck was awarded a sale on Trout Lake Creek. And R. B. Norris was awarded a fir sale in the Beaver Creek area in 1945.

"The first power saw to be used by District people was a 12 HP two—cylinder Titan with a 5 or 6 foot bar and stinger. A real beast. Several had been purchased by the Regional Office and shipped to selected Districts for evaluation. Apparently there was some doubt as to their practicability. It weighed about 120 pounds, so its over—the-shoulder mobility was restricted. Hollenbeck and Broughton at this time were still hand—sawing, but Neils was using some electric saws powered by generators mounted on old crawler tractors."

—Bob Larse, 1989 letter

"Finally, on April 1, 1945 I moved to Randle. The timber resource of the district was being developed as rapidly as possible to meet the demands of the War effort... When I arrived, all sales were assigned to me... All the rapid expansion brought with it some serious problems. We didn't have adequate maps at the start. Maps had been developed from aerial photos as fast as the Region could move on them. We didn't have time to train people in sale layout and administration. Because of the railroad access to the Iron Cr. area we had no competitive bidding on the timber. The Kosmos Timber Co.

END OF AN ERA: LOADING LOGS ON RAIL CARS, J. NEILS LUMBER COMANY TIMBER SALE NEAR MOUNT ADAMS, ONE OF THE LAST RAILROAD LOGGING OPERATIONS ON THE FOREST

was starting to truck log but the roads all came in to a railhead where the logs were transferred to railroad cars before being hauled out of Iron Cr. We had no housing for increased numbers of timber sale personnel... Work accomplishment in Iron Creek was difficult. A typical work day consisted of arising about 4:30 a.m., driving 16 miles to Kosmos and catching the speeder at the logging camp. Arriving at the railhead about 8: 00 a.m. we still had to travel by company log truck or pickup on the logging roads. Often it was 9:00 or 10:00 a.m. before we started work. At about 3:30 p.m. we would drop

---

LOAD OF LOGS FROM IRON CREEK TIMBER SALE, CROSSING COWLITZ RIVER, 1949

everything and run for the speeder. We would arrive home around 6 or 7:00 p.m. On sale layout work Jim and I would work out of a backpack camp well beyond the truck road development."

—*H. C. Chriswell, Randle District Ranger, 1945-1950,* MEMOIRS, *1989*

"In the Douglas-fir region, because of the large size of the timber, combined at times with rough topography and swampy ground, the general practice has been to clear cut in logging. This consists of falling and bucking all timber of merchantable size, usually 16 inches d.b.h. and over. The logs are then pulled by donkey engine to a central point for loading on railroad cars or trucks. Much of the remaining small timber is knocked down in this process. Finally, in order to abate the fire hazard, the slash is burned broadcast, which, for the most part, kills any standing trees that may be left unless special protection is given them."

COWLITZ TIMBER MANAGEMENT PLAN, *1948*

"We were personally part of the change as our administration moved from custodianship by the 'old timers' to scientific management under an increasing and heavy use of the resources. Along with this came the strong controversies over their use. Our decisions became increasingly difficult. We bravely hung onto the direction of our first Chief who long ago wrote, 'The greatest good for the greatest number in the long run,' establishing the multiple use concept. That meant something important to us in the field."

—*H. C. Chriswell, Randle District Ranger, 1945-1950,* MEMOIRS, *1989*

THE HOOD RIVER COUNCIL OF BOY SCOUTS MAINTAINED AN ORGANIZATION CAMP AT BIRD LAKE IN THE 1930S. APPROXIMATELY SIXTY BOYS AND SIXTY GIRLS WERE BROUGHT THERE EVERY SUMMER TO PURSUE WOODCRAFT, GEOLOGY, BOTANY, SWIMMING, AND BOATING

DEVELOPED RECREATION SITE IMPROVEMENTS, LA WIS WIS FOREST CAMP

CAMPERS CHECK IN AT NORTH FORK GUARD STATION

Recreation

Recreation use of the forest declined during World War II, due in large part to gasoline rationing. After the war, however, recreation use jumped to a figure much greater than pre-war visits. The remarkable increase in recreation led Congress to pass a special appropriation for 1947 to restore and improve existing recreation facilities. In 1949, fees were charged for recreation facility use for the first time in the history of the forest: fifty cents to camp or picnic in developed recreation sites.

In 1948 there were approximately 31,000 recreational visitors to Spirit Lake. In 1949 the Portland YMCA, Longview YMCA, Portland Area Girl Scouts, Portland and Cowlitz County Boy Scouts, St. Helens Mountaineer Club, and Longview News Carriers all maintained organization camps at Spirit Lake. Skiing became popular in the period 1936-1938. An organization site for winter sports was also developed at the base of Mount St. Helens.

Camping, hiking, mountain climbing, fishing, and berry picking were the major recreational activities on the forest. In 1938 there were more than 20,000 acres of huckleberry fields in the Twin Buttes country alone.

Noted for its abundant wildflowers, waterfalls, and scenic beauty, the area around Bird Creek Meadows saw construction of campgrounds in 1935.

DEVELOPMENTS AT LA WIS WIS FOREST CAMP INCLUDED RUSTIC SWINGS, FLUSH TOILETS, AND A PICNIC SHELTER

PACKWOOD LAKE, WITH JOHNSON PEAK IN THE DISTANCE

CORNELIA PINCHOT, LYLE WATTS, AND WASHINGTON GOVERNOR ARTHUR LANGLIE SPEAKING AT MONUMENT DEDICATION, LA WIS WIS FOREST CAMP

Renaming and Dedication

Gifford Pinchot died in 1946 at the age of 81. Soon after his death, Lyle Watts, chief of the U. S. Forest Service, together with Charles Brannan, Secretary of Agriculture, mounted an effort to have one of the national forests renamed for the father of the U. S. Forest Service. Columbia National Forest received the honor because of "its importance and in recognition of the fact that the area is one of the top forests in the United States." The decision process involved discussion with K. P. Cecil and "various old timers and prominent citizens" in Clark County and throughout the state. By 1948, Washington's congressional delegation was also involved in this process and went on record supporting the name change. President Harry Truman signed the proclamation redesignating Columbia National Forest as Gifford Pinchot National Forest on June 15, 1949. Initially, there was some grumbling among the residents of communities surrounding the national forest. An editorial in one newspaper read: "…no matter what kind of official name the forest may bear, it will always be the Columbia National Forest, so long as one of the present generation may survive." Most of the public, however, quickly accepted the name.

A formal dedication ceremony was held October 15, 1949 at La Wis Wis Forest Camp, near Packwood. Addressing the assembled crowd were Cornelia Pinchot,

DEDICATION

OF

GIFFORD PINCHOT NATIONAL FOREST

STATE OF WASHINGTON

OCTOBER 15, 1949

LA WIS WIS FOREST CAMP

UNDER THE AUSPICES OF
UNITED STATES FOREST SERVICE
AND
SOCIETY OF AMERICAN FORESTERS

COVER OF PROGRAM FROM 1949 DEDICATION CEREMONY

widow of Gifford Pinchot; U.S. Forest Service Chief Lyle Watts; Washington Governor Arthur Langlie; Gifford Pinchot National Forest Supervisor Kirk P. Cecil; and Clyde Martin, president of the Society of American Foresters. H. J. Andrews, Regional Forester, Pacific Northwest Region, U. S. Forest Service presided over the ceremony and introduced the speakers. The speech given by Lyle Watts was particularly moving and most quoted in the newspapers. In concluding, he said:

"Our entire National Forest system, embracing more than 180 million acres in the United States and its territories, is, in a large sense, a monument to Gifford Pinchot. But to this beautiful forest here in the Cascades of Washington has come the special honor of bearing his name. This National Forest was established when he was chief forester. Its administration began under his direction. The basic principles for its management were set up under his guidance.

LYLE WATTS SPEAKING AT DEDICATION CEREMONY, LA WIS WIS FOREST CAMP

May the Gifford Pinchot National Forest help to keep forever alive and dynamic his conservation ideals. May it help point the way to wise use of all forests and all resources in the attainment of the good life for all men and all nations."

> —Lyle Watts, U.S. Forest Service Chief, in a 1949
> speech at La Wis Wis Forest Camp

The name of the Columbia National Forest has this date been changed by proclamation of President Truman from Columbia, to Gifford Pinchot National Forest. This is in recognition and in honor of the first professional Forester and first Chief of the Forest Service who initiated action and focused attention upon the need for forest conservation in the United States."

> —K. P. Cecil, Forest Supervisor, June 15, 1949, press release

"In dedicating the Gifford Pinchot National Forest today, we honor one of America's great men. It was Gifford Pinchot who gave conservation its first great impetus in the United States. It was largely through his tireless crusading efforts that conservation has become a part of our national policy. The ideas and forces that Gifford Pinchot set in motion may well determine the future security and prosperity and progress of this Nation. They may indeed determine the future welfare of the entire human race.

There are many among us here today who knew and worked with 'G.P.,' as Gifford Pinchot was familiarly and affectionately known to all his associates. They remember G.P. as a man of tremendous energy and enthusiasm, as an inspiring leader, as a zealous crusader. They knew him as a courageous, unflinching fighter in the public interest and for the public good. His cause did not need to be popular if it was right. He seemed at times to be fighting almost single-handed; but history has shown that the people were behind him."

> —Lyle Watts, Chief Forester, U.S. Forest Service, from
> text of address at Oct. 15, 1949 dedication

Historic Sites and Interpretive Trails

Several popular interpretive trails and historic sites that can be visited by the public on Gifford Pinchot National Forest are indicated with asterisks on the map below, and shown at opposite.

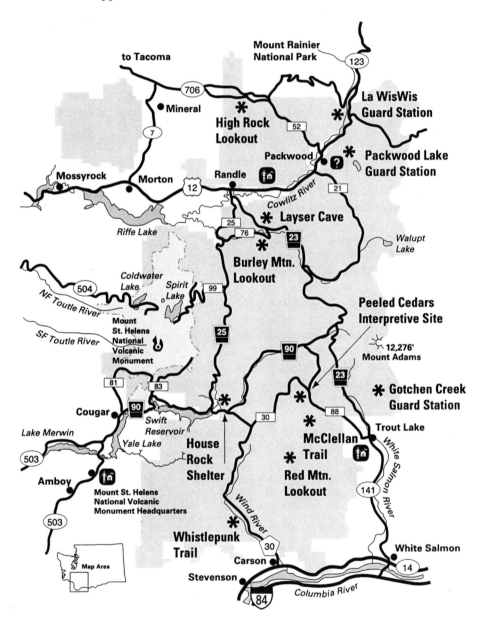

HIGH ROCK FIRE LOOKOUT

LA WIS WIS GUARD STATION

PACKWOOD LAKE GUARD STATION

BURLEY MOUNTAIN LOOKOUT

LAYSER CAVE

MCCLELLAN TRAIL

RED MOUNTAIN LOOKOUT

GOTCHEN CREEK GUARD STATION

WHISTLEPUNK TRAIL

PEELED CEDAR TREES, MOUNT ADAMS DISTRICT

Credits

Maps

Helga Christiansen, geometronics, Gifford Pinchot National Forest: 5, 96

National Archives and Records Center, Seattle: 29

U.S. Department of the Interior, Geological Survey: 22

Art and Illustrations

Editorial cartoon, courtesy *The Columbian*: 72

Book cover courtesy MacMillan and Co.: 85

Four Clackama Indians, Paul Kane, courtesy Stark Museum of Art, Orange, Texas: 11

Poster, courtesy Gerald W. Williams: 19

Photographs

All photos courtesy USDA Forest Service, Gifford Pinchot National Forest Heritage Program Collections except the following:

Courtesy of Ivy Beck: 59

Courtesy of Ben Langfield: 6

Library of Congress, Washington, D. C.: 12

Courtesy of Louis Lorengel: 87

Courtesy of The Mountaineers: 68

Courtesy of Hugh Vogel: 48

Grey Towers National Historic Landmark: vi, 83, 84

Chester Vanderpool: 10

U.S. Department of the Interior, Geological Survey: 21

USDA Forest Service, Mount Baker-Snoqualmie National Forest, Heritage Program Collections: 27, 55, 56, 60, 64

USDA Forest Service, Washington Office History Program: 61, 69, 76

Book Design

Ben Nechanicky, Northwest Interpretive Association, adapted from previous design by MacKay

Additional Reading

Guggenheim, Alan. *Spirit Lake People.* (Gresham, OR: Salem Press, 1986.)

Hardy, Martha. *Tatoosh.* (Seattle, WA: The Mountaineers, 1980).

Herring, Margaret and Sarah Greene. *Forest of Time: A Century of Science at Wind River Experimental Forest.* (Oregon State University Press, 2007.)

Hill, Edwin. *In the Shadow of the Mountain.* (Pullman, WA, Washington State University Press, 1990.)

Kresek, Ray. *Fire Lookouts of the Pacific Northwest.* (Spokane, WA: Ye Galleon Press, 1998.)

McCoy, Keith. *The Mount Adams Country: Forgotten Corner of the Columbia River Gorge.* White Salmon, WA: Pahto Publications,1987.)

Pinchot, Gifford. *Breaking New Ground.* (New York, NY: Harcourt, Brace and Co., 1947.) (reprinted 1972, University of Washington Press)

Spring, Ira and Byron Fish. *Firewatchers of the Cascades and Olympics.* (Seattle, WA: The Mountaineers, 1997.)

Steen, Harold K. *The U. S. Forest Service: A History.* (Seattle, WA: University of Washington Press, 1991.)

FOREST SUPERVISOR K. P. CECIL AND HIS WIFE ALWILDA AT THE 1949 DEDICATION CEREMONY AT

Gifford Pinchot National Forest Statistics — 1949

Number recreationists —
campers, picnickers, and hikers visiting forest in 1948 163,500

Number improved forest camps 82

Annual timber cut calendar year 1948 .... 93 Million Ft. B. M.

Number sheep grazed annually 6,600

Number cattle grazed annually 1,200

Expenditures fiscal year 1948 (appropriated funds) $348,000

Receipts distributed to 6 southwestern
Washington Counties in 1948 .... $161,767

Number yearlong employees 60

Number seasonal employees 200

Number ranger districts 6

(Mount Adams, Lewis River, Randle, Wind River, Spirit Lake, Packwood)

Forest roads .... 655 miles

Forest trails .... 2,101 miles

Telephone lines .... 843 miles

Fire lookouts 50

Guard stations 25

Gifford Pinchot National Forest Statistics — 2008

Number recreationists —
campers, picnickers and hikers visiting forest in 2007 ...1,800,000

Number improved forest camps... 54

Annual timber cut fiscal year 2007 .... 13.24 Million Ft. B.M.

Number sheep grazed annually 0

Number cattle grazed annually........................696 cow/calf pairs

Expenditures fiscal year 2007 (appropriated funds) $21,613,826

Receipts distributed to 6 southwestern
Washington Counties in 1998...............................$16,586,394

Recreation Fee Demo returns in 1998....................... $1,239,755

Number yearlong employees 160

Number seasonal employees 60

Number ranger districts.. 3

(Mount Adams, Cowlitz Valley, Mount St. Helens National Volcanic Monument)

Forest roads .... 4,105 miles

Forest trails .... 1,475 miles

Telephone lines.............. 9 miles

Fire lookouts 4

Guard stations 8

MOUNT ADAMS DISTRICT RANGER K. C. LANGFIELD IN THE FIELD, 1940s

Breinigsville, PA USA
04 September 2009
223571BV00001B/1/P